Newly Widowed, Now Socially Awkward

Facing Interpersonal Challenges After Loss

Eileen L. Cooley, Ph.D.

Newly Widowed, Now Socially Awkward
Facing Interpersonal Challenges After Loss

Editing and writer's coaching:
Wayne South Smith, www.waynesouthsmith.com

Interior page design:
Jera Publishing, www.jerapublishing.com

Cover Design:
Laura Nalesnik

Author Photo:
Judy Kuniansky Photography, Atlanta

Library of Congress Control Number: 2017900775

ISBN: 978-0-9984778-0-0

Published by:
ELCooley Publishing
Atlanta, Georgia, USA

To Dave, With Love

Contents

Foreword

I WAS FORCED to embark on an unplanned, difficult journey.

When I lost my husband a few years ago, I was lost myself, filled with pain, disbelief, and confusion. My life was derailed, and I could not imagine tolerating the ongoing grief. As I put one foot in front of the other, barely remembering the first six months, I continued to feel adrift.

To help me manage the misery, I read lots of books about becoming and being a widow. Many provided helpful advice—for example, "Don't make major changes right away"—and some offered hope that over time my feelings would become more manageable. A few offered glimpses of how my daily life might change and I would eventually come out the other side. However, none really addressed my changing social interactions.

As a new widow, I expected to lean on my adult children, relatives, and friends, saw a therapist, and never thought about the time-limited nature of sympathy. I was not anticipating social disappointments, but somehow they came with the territory. I wondered how much my sad mood was biasing my viewpoint.

After a while I realized I had become socially unsure. The script of who I was—a woman with a husband and a shared home—was gone and with it many of my automatic responses. My interpersonal interactions now required thought and more effort. Often I did not know what I wanted. I had to think about how to respond to invitations and what to do when I was alone without any. I had to think more about how to behave with groups of people, and, of course, think more about how to manage my time alone. I had to decide when it was acceptable to share strong feelings about my loss and when my best course of action was to bring up only lighter topics or stay focused on others. I had lost my social anchor, part of my social identity, and seemingly, some of my fluid social skills.

Nevertheless I was caught off-guard by my own feelings of aggravation at other people. Internally I bristled when they did not say the right thing or failed to say something useful. Some told me "time heals all" or some other platitude that was more of an irritant than a help. Unexpectedly, the list of awkward situations and aggravations continued to grow: they introduced me as a widow, failed to include me, forgot the new important dates in my life, told me they knew how I felt, and generally assumed I'd be back on my feet after a year.

At the same time I started to notice my own social errors. Sometimes I would apologize right away for sharing too much grief or being too moody, and other times I would realize my interpersonal mistakes after I was back home. When preoccupied with my own grief, I didn't always listen as well to others, responded unhappily to social invitations, sought too much sympathy, sometimes negated offers of support, and shared the most negative side of myself with my closest friends.

I am not sure if the irritations I felt with other people—and still feel sometimes—were justified, but I decided to write about them anyway. I found it useful to record my thoughts, and composing these essays helped me manage my negative feelings and subsequently my reactions. My unpleasant thoughts and feelings contributed to my downward spirals, and writing helped me neutralize these. At the same time, I also wanted to examine and try to correct my own social errors. Surely I couldn't blame others for their comments and behaviors without examining my own role as well. Most of the needed changes were definitely up to me, and I wanted to become more of an advocate for myself. Writing about how to cope with these situations helped me to get through them.

Social aggravations also were a safer topic. As I analyzed my annoyance with others and my own emotional variability, I could avoid some of my overwhelming grief. It was usually too difficult to write about the loss itself, but having a tinge of anger seemed to help somehow. I knew there were better ways to relate to new widows than how I was being handled, how I was handling myself, and how I had previously responded to others who had suffered loss. I decided to address how we, the ones left behind, may help ourselves when confronting these uncomfortable situations. Thus, the concept of this book was born.

I wrote this book with a blend of two voices. The first voice, filled with raw emotions, is my voice as a widow, the personal voice of disbelief and pain. This is the voice that is sometimes disappointed in others while at the same time clinging to them. The second voice represents my perspective as a psychologist, a voice that attempts to offer slightly more objective observations. I try to view my social dilemmas from a distance as I attempt to handle uncomfortable interpersonal situations. Sometimes, however, I could not find a course of action, and I had to convince myself to simply accept the awkwardness.

This book is divided into three sections to reflect my phases of grief and social readjustment: "In the Beginning," "After a While," and "Over Time." As I move along in this journey, I can see myself changing from mostly raw emotions to emotions mixed with more and more thoughts and logic. I am becoming more rational and less often stuck. Of course, we all have different experiences and time frames. Each essay addresses how I experienced a situation and concludes with some ideas on "What I can do for myself." These essays may be read in any order, as each one represents a specific set of circumstances.

You may notice inconsistencies both within and between essays as I experienced my own emotions.

I know our friends and relatives—our sources of support—have only positive intentions as they try to meet some of our needs. They have their lives to live and cannot spend time walking on eggshells around us, their grieving and less predictable widowed friends. Therefore, it is mostly up to us to work toward finding and giving ourselves the support we need as we face uncertainty and tackle tremendous loneliness.

I hope my thoughts and feelings may be helpful to you. Some essays may be similar to your experiences, and some are uniquely mine. I lost my husband when I was in my early 60s, after almost 30 years of marriage. I was still working, and my children were grown and out of the house. I did not have the strain of raising children alone that many women face. I also was in a friendship circle with mostly married couples, and this too impacted my experiences as I tried to socialize without the support of other singles.

The essence of the interactions and situations in this book are real. I was reporting my experiences as they occurred, although sometimes I wrote the full essay itself several months later. Please note I have changed the names and relationships of the people involved and have altered the details of the interpersonal situations to protect the identities of others.

As widows and survivors of profound loss, we are confronting major lifestyle changes. I hope we can take better care of ourselves when we're alone, add understanding to our awkward social interactions, and learn to more directly ask for what we want and need from the important people in our lives.

Wishing all of us peace in the journey ahead.

Eileen Cooley

PART ONE

In the Beginning

THE ESSAYS IN this first section were written during the first few months while I was trying desperately to get a grip on my loss. I was sad, depressed, and lonely much of the time and sometimes irritated with other people and the new situations I faced. I was looking at life through a lens of misery that seemed to negatively impact my social interactions. I was generally feeling sorry for myself. I started monitoring my comments to avoid leaking this extreme pessimism and tried to maintain some neutrality in my conversations. As a result of these efforts, I often felt exhausted after leaving a social interaction.

This was not the phase in which I wanted to interact with new people as I was too forlorn. I was often numb and tuned-out. I am lucky, and now grateful, that my close friends and relatives hung in there with me, as I know I was not always easy to be with. I said a lot of "yes-buts" in response to the suggestions of

1

others and often secretly decided they just could not relate to my grief. The most useful support I received was help with concrete tasks, receiving invitations for dinner or coffee—whether or not I accepted—and when someone simply accompanied me on a walk or went to a movie with me.

1

"Call Me if You Need Anything"

Marie, walking out the door, says, "Call me if you need anything."

*I talk briefly with Grace in the grocery store. "Call me anytime,"
she says as she hugs me goodbye.*

I CAN'T BEGIN to count the number of times people have said
this to me. I hear it in person, of course, but also in condolence
notes, on the phone, in emails, and even in texts. If I bump
into someone I haven't seen in a while, they may add, "Give
me a call so we can get together" or "I'm always here for you."

Well, after such a major life trauma, I am *less* likely than
ever to be the initiator. I am overwhelmed and depressed, missing my husband, and trying to fathom how my life is forever
changed. In this state of profound sadness and drained energy,
reaching out is harder, not easier, in spite of my increased needs

for help and contact. I find it difficult to even think about all the things I want or need, and it makes it more stressful for the ball to be tossed into my lap. I don't want my interactions, at this point in time, to rise or fall based on *my* initiations. If they do, I may end up with very few contacts.

I don't think these statements bothered me before I lost my husband. In fact, I know I have said this phrase over and over without realizing how it sounded. I meant it just like my friends do now. I was willing and wanting to be helpful but wasn't sure what to do, wasn't sure what the other person needed.

People have good intentions when they say these words. They are on unsure ground just like I am. They just don't have a sense of where to begin. They don't know what to do or say; none of us do. Most of my friends have not lost a close friend or certainly not their partner. Although many have lost parents, losing a partner or spouse has distinctly different consequences. I feel like I'm lost at sea without a guide.

The words "call me" may also reflect their awkwardness and avoidance. They can't imagine what it must be like and don't really want to think about it. To be with me, they'd have to put themselves in my shoes. Who wants to do that? We all are aging along with our partners and each one fears the outcome I am living. Many people have told me that now they worry more about losing their partner. So I understand if, for some people, there is a hint of avoidance underlying their request for me to call them, rather than vice versa.

So what's the answer? What do I want, and are there any "correct" words? I wanted, and still want, others to initiate, to call, to stop by, and to make specific offers. I will forever appreciate the friend who came to the funeral home with me, the colleague who called at 5 p.m. and stated, "Come eat with us tonight," the friend who wrote thank-you notes for the charitable donations, or the neighbor who drove me to the airport.

In reality, nobody can help me with the bigger issues of how to survive without my partner or how to understand why he suddenly became ill and died. But they can help with the smaller, daily stresses of eating alone and going alone. I want others to replace "Call me" with "I'll call you tomorrow." And to do it, if they can.

What I can do for myself:

When I hear "Call me if you need anything," I can reframe it in my mind as "I want to help but don't know how." Then I can say, "Please call me next week. I can't think what I need right now." This gives us both time. Or, to be really honest, I could say, "I'm too overwhelmed to make phone calls, so it would be easier if you call me when you have time."

2

Don't Introduce Me as a Widow

I ring her doorbell, and Mary greets me. "Hey, come on in. Let me introduce you to my friend Sarah. She's been widowed for three or four years now. Hey, Sarah, here is my friend I told you about who's a new widow."

I am walking with Sandra, and we see a friend of hers. Sandra says, "Oh, hi! Nice to see you again, Joan. I know you finalized your divorce last year." She smiles at me, then turns to Joan, "Meet my friend here who lost her husband a few months ago. Unfortunately, I expect you two have a lot in common."

I HATE BEING introduced as a widow. I used to be a neighbor, a colleague, a relative, a friend, or simply introduced by my name. Now all of these labels are often relegated to second place, and my "widow" title gets top billing.

Besides being annoyed with the widow introduction, I feel embarrassed to now have this label. I often want to hide this fact from my peers and certainly from myself. I have lost part of my identity now, and being widowed suggests sadness and lack of connection. It reminds me my life is limited; it highlights my loss.

If I don't tell others I am a widow, I can hold on to the illusion that I'm not alone. I would rather stay married in my mind and ignore reality. Such introductory remarks thrust me out of my imaginary hideaway. Being introduced as a widow provides personal information that I'm not ready to face.

I understand how we categorize other people in terms of relationships. We describe others by whether they are single or divorced, have children or not. We use these groupings to find commonalities. For example, we frequently discuss our children when talking with other parents. Similarly, complaining about the ups and downs of dating might be an acceptable topic for a group of single friends. However, the newly widowed might not enjoy their new grouping or the topics that go along with it. Being a widow does not mean I want to discuss widowhood or loss. It is definitely not in the same category as sharing about my children or my career.

I introduce myself in different ways to different people in different situations. Sometimes, I go without labels. I want to meet new people without preconceived notions. I don't want to be pegged by my career or my marital status.

Instead, I might share my interest in the food being served, a recent movie, the antics of my dogs, or an informative story I heard on public radio. I don't want my remarks to be filtered through my personal labels, either positively or negatively. More often, I want to learn about new people by what *they choose* to share.

In contrast, there are other occasions when I do want to share about my loss. In the right context and when I'm in the right frame of mind, I welcome hearing about how other people are tackling difficult adjustments now that their children have left home, their spouse lost a job, their parents are aging, or they have experienced an illness or loss. For example, in a small gathering of friends, the conversation may shift to this deeper level of personal disclosure. In this context, sharing my adjustment to being a widow may be just what I need.

So I've just contradicted myself. There are, in fact, times when I want to tell others that I'm a widow.

So what is the real problem with the "widow" introduction? It bothers me that others are deciding *what* I share and *when* I share it. When they introduce me as a widow, they are taking away my choice and assuming my readiness. I want them to leave it up to me. I may announce that I am a widow, or I may choose to keep it to myself. I want the timing and the details to be mine.

Of course I realize when friends announce my widowhood to other people, they are trying to be helpful. My friends want me to feel less isolated and less alone. They want to help me meet others who may share similar problems.

Although this may be helpful for me, the "widow" introduction is best left to me.

What I can do for myself:

When my widowhood becomes part of the introduction before I'm ready, I may need to pause for a minute to steady myself. Then, as I gather my emotions and return to the present, I can steer the conversation in another direction. I can ask the other people about themselves or comment on another topic. I don't have to stay with the widow topic.

Over time, I know I'll get better at redirecting conversations, and, of course, I'll be more accepting of my loss.

3

You Were There at the Funeral;
Where Are You Now?

THE CHAPEL WAS packed. I didn't even see all the people who were there. Entering through the side door and sitting in the front row, I hardly looked around. People came from my job, his job, and from the many places we belonged—from the YMCA to the neighborhood. Friends and relatives from both near and far came to pay their respects.

I felt surrounded by community. I am glad that so many attended the memorial service and saw the slide show featuring his wide grin, his love of nature and family, his enthusiasm for adventure, and his obvious optimism. After the service, there were kind words and warm hugs. Similarly at home, my children and I were inundated with flowers, fruit, condolence cards, and guests.

I was therefore surprised by how fast the divisions happened. After the funeral, my world was suddenly split into camps: those who kept in touch and remained part of my life, distant friends who suddenly made more efforts to keep in touch, those who initiated occasional check-ins, and those who never contacted me again.

I suppose I really didn't know about these factions right away. I certainly was not keeping a checklist of who called and who stopped by. However after several months, when I had too much time on my hands, I started to notice. I thought it was strange that Sally and Bob hadn't called or odd that I hadn't heard from Cathy in so long.

Perhaps it really was simply a contrast effect. I am lucky in many ways; I have several close friends who regularly keep in touch. We keep track of the ups and downs of each other's daily lives, and this pattern continued after my loss. We may have even become closer after his death. I also have immediate family members that I regularly speak to, and these relationships also continued.

Then there were those casual friends who made more effort to stay in touch and offer support. A few people who I had previously seen only once every few months, or spoke to long distance, called more often. I still appreciate when they think of me, email me, or call me.

But what about the others? There are couples my husband and I knew who have rarely called, relatives who have become scarce, and casual friends who must have dropped off the planet. I attempt to figure out what they are thinking and how to interpret their absence from my life.

Perhaps some of us were social friends only as couples. Therefore, with my partner gone, the four-some or six-some just can't happen. They may not think in odd numbers, and they may assume the configuration is no longer possible. They may not be backing away; they may simply be accepting the reality that our couples-based friendship has ended.

Other absentees may have thought, and perhaps still think, that I need space to process my grief. I have always disliked it when others assume I need space and give it to me without asking. I don't usually need time alone and, in fact, I often work through my problems best through dialogue. In hard times, I seek closeness. When worried or unhappy, I seek companionship and camaraderie. However, I know this is not true for everyone, so perhaps those who stayed away are giving me what they might need: space to heal. Perhaps they will slowly come back into my life. They may reappear. I will have to wait and see.

Still others who are distant may simply be avoiders of the topics of death and loss, those who simply do not wish to be associated with me, the person in grief. They may find me, and the widowhood I stand for, too unpleasant for regular contact. I may remind them of other deaths they have endured and other sources of sadness. They may associate me with the possibility of their own future losses.

13

In spite of all these explanations, however, I must cope with absences from my life that I can't explain. I don't know what they are thinking or feeling. A few times I initiated contact with someone who had "vanished," and I heard, "I've been meaning to call you but..." They were nice and kind when they answered the phone but somehow more awkward in responding to me. I am not sure why, and each one may have unique reasons I just don't know about.

In any case, I am left with a new pattern of relationships—some closer and some unexpectedly more distant. I had not anticipated any pull-aways, so these additional losses have required readjustment on my part.

What I can do for myself:

I can keep a balanced perspective and not get caught up in the reasons others pull back or do not reach out. I must keep working to stop myself from feeling shut out or rejected. I am missing too much information to really know why I am not hearing from other people.

Instead, I want to relish the relationships that have improved and try to avoid bitterness for those I may have lost by remembering the good things from our history together.

4

"Take It One Day at a Time"

I bump into an old friend at the drug store who has recently heard about my loss. She says, "I heard your awful news. I know these first few months will be really hard. But keep reminding yourself to just take it one day at a time."

I'm at a neighborhood meeting when my neighbor Jackie comes up to me to catch up. After I share the news about my husband, she says, "How awful. Just remember you will get stronger each day."

THE PHRASES PEOPLE often use for comfort are not really comforting. I hold my breath and sort of clench my fists when I hear one coming. Sometimes I think I can even see one coming. I picture wide eyes under a furrowed brow, a pursed-lipped smile, and a voice whispering in my ear, "Let's not talk about this too much."

In a typical scenario, other people hear the news of my loss, pause ever so briefly when not knowing what to say, and then, with a hardly noticeable sigh of relief, offer a phrase or two like, "You can get through this," or "I know this is really difficult but remember you've been through tough situations before." As they speak, they look at me with sad but understanding eyes, as if I could take in their support by osmosis. The moment passes and the conversation shifts to common topics such as work or politics. The earlier phrases are left to dissipate into the air, leaving only a dusty residue that I'll brush off myself later.

I do get it; I know other people mean well. These potentially soothing phrases are part of our social scripts of what to say in the face of another person's loss. They make up our repertoire when we become caught in a moment of bad news. When we can say one of these sentences, we are relieved to have something to say, able to offer condolences with a way out of the awkwardness. And, of course, as perhaps is true for all social scripts, there is some truth in those words. It's just that those stock phrases appear to be simply canned, somewhat empty responses to me, the person who has recently endured a loss and is feeling lost.

What is it really like for me? My pain seems endless, intense, and hopeless. While I know in my head that time marches on and, in fact, in the future I probably will be doing different things, thinking different thoughts, and feeling different emotions, my current state of mind finds that reality hard to fathom.

Sometimes, I cannot picture the next day, much less the future. I hear these phrases as if they were meant for someone else, not for me. No, I tell myself, they won't work for me. Perhaps mine will remain an open wound instead of a healed one.

Of course I can't share this level of discouragement in the midst of most social encounters. If I did, I would drive people away. I need to pretend the statements are not bothering me and, in fact, provide a measure of hope. So I bottle up my grief for the sake of smoother conversation.

While these social phrases may indeed offer words of truth, the irony is that they are more likely to be valued much later on, after the grief has lessened and much more time has passed. It is true that taking it one day at a time is indeed the way to keep going. However, this phrase needs to be paired with time spent sitting in grief.

I think less is more in responding to grief. I find "Oh no," or "How terrible" easier to swallow. These phrases offer less hope, but also less pressure to clean up and move on. They give me permission to tell a little more, to provide a few more details that are fighting to be released. I then can watch to see if the other people are hanging in there with me, willing to hear a little more of my experience. If they are, I may continue a bit, and, if not, I can then change the subject.

However, over these first few months I have heard the typical go-to phrases so often that they are now my cue to move on. Like the lines of an actor on stage, I hear the words and automatically respond with my next act. The phrase instructs me to smile gently, thank them for their kindness, and then graciously switch the topic. I let both of us off the hook.

What I can do for myself:

I cannot change the social scripts we all lean on in times of uncertainty or difficulty. I know when these phrases are uttered that they represent awkwardness, not unkindness. I want to pay attention to the attempt at helpfulness, not the words attached to it. I want to stop feeling annoyed when other people say the "wrong" things.

In some circumstances, I can let other people know that it is too soon for me to take in these ideas. I can say, "I know in my head what you are saying is probably true, but it just doesn't feel that way right now. It is all still too raw for me."

I hope the next time I am looking into the eyes of a grieving friend that I will remember not to say these phrases and instead just be quiet and acknowledge his or her intense sorrow.

5

Asking for Help Too Often

"Can you drive me to the auto shop on Friday? I need to pick up my car."

"Will you go with me to the safe deposit box this week? I dread seeing what's inside."

"Do you have time to talk? I really need to talk this one out. Oh, sorry, I didn't realize it's so late."

EVEN WITH PEOPLE saying "Call me if you need me," I hate asking for help, and now, as a widow, I am forced to ask more often than ever. I ask for assistance for particular tasks, like rides to the airport or carrying the 30-pound bag of dog food inside. I ask for help for emotional issues and decisions too, like accompaniment to the courthouse or deciding what to do with my retirement accounts. I feel slightly terrified for the time when I urgently need someone, such as the unexpected middle-of-the-night appendectomy when nobody is here.

I worry about using up my requests and burning out my close friends. I go to unrealistic extremes, worrying that they may stop answering the phone and start ignoring my texts. I envision an invisible quota and the penalty I might face if I violate the numbers. Too many calls are equal to a small fine. Too many requests for rides equals a medium fine. Too many calls for quick action equals a fairly large fine. Of course the fines would not be money but less contact, fewer invitations, or simply an unwanted hesitation. Even if these fines are totally in my imagination, risking the reality of being rejected is too high a price to pay after my loss.

In my mind it is not just the number of requests that matters. Frequency within a given time period is important too. How many requests have I already made this month to the same person? How many times this week did I ask her for a ride? Another driver ran into my car in a parking lot soon after my husband died. This required several rides to the repair shop, and I found that making these requests made me anxious. What if my car breaks down again and I have to ask for two rides in one day?

Inconvenience also plays into the picture. What if my car breaks down after 9 p.m.? What if I schedule a flight too early in the morning? Is the other person too tired that night but feels obligated to help? Was my friend in the middle of something more interesting or more important when I called? An inconvenient request might equal two or even three convenient ones. How can I tell? When will I know?

Perhaps I need a spreadsheet or a new app for my cell phone to calculate my "favor usage" for each month, maybe even each week. I wonder if it would be like the electricity or the gas bill. How much did I use that month, and what is the charge? What if increased usage results in an exponentially increased bill? I just don't know the mathematical function or when there may be a rapid debt accumulation. I must proceed with caution.

When my husband was here, the daily tasks were, of course, no-brainers. He did the heavy work I could not manage, and he always picked me up at the airport. He lugged in the large bag of dog food, mowed the lawn, changed the ceiling light bulbs, and together we turned over the mattress. He also took care of many of the regular household tasks. He stopped at the store for milk, washed the dishes, and did the laundry.

As I transition to being widowed, I am struck by all of the advantages of having a go-to person at home. Without the special-person-for-me, I am left with a stack of requests, each of which requires more planning and advance coordination. The hassles of everyday life have become increasingly frustrating. As an overwhelmed widow, I must now ask others for favors and then another one, and alas one more. As most of my friends have their own driver, I dislike the one-way street I'm creating.

I feel tremendous relief when someone offers specific help and I do not have to ask.

For discussing major personal decisions I've always relied on my friends in addition to my husband, so at first I thought this area would be more manageable even with the loss. But I was wrong. With my increased tension, I feel more desperate for input than ever before. My confidence in my own decision-making ability has become shaky at best. I want more consultation than is reasonable to ask. Even the simple decisions now seem more difficult. It is a question of volume, time, and perceived burden. Again the quota problem of how much, how often, and how inconvenient rears its ugly head.

When I was able to consult with my husband, I was more flexible and relaxed in my requests to others. Since he was available, I could more easily delay my needs, and I felt less urgent. Now my sense of timing and urgency are distorted.

Of course I realize I am simply experiencing the world the way single people have always experienced it. I was on my own before too, but somehow this is different. When I was single before, most everyone else I knew was single, so asking each other for help was a common exchange. Now, with most of my friends married, I have to ask them, but they don't have to ask me. I am sensitive to this imbalance.

What I can do for myself:

For some heavy, physical tasks, I can exercise more patience. I usually can wait until another person stops by who can join me in lifting or moving.

For my ride requests, I have altered my patterns to use the transit system and off-site airport parking services. I now have my car repaired in a neighborhood shop I can walk to. When I really still need a ride, I just bite the bullet and ask, trying to ask in advance to minimize inconvenience.

I know I will adapt and get more comfortable with these new strategies. I increasingly get advice from the employees at the hardware store and have learned to use YouTube for minor fix-it problems. For example, I felt pride after following an online video to fix my garbage disposal.

Although it is true that I cannot always reciprocate in kind for my friends, I remind myself that there are other ways to exchange helpfulness, other ways to be a good friend. I can let myself out of the quid-pro-quo mindset.

6

TMI: Why Am I Telling Strangers?

"I need to change our mortgage so only my name is on the house. You see my husband recently died and . . ."

"I've been needing a haircut. I delayed making this appointment, as I was too upset to deal with it. After I lost my husband, I seemed to put many things on hold."

"I need you to come fix the lights in the back of my house. Ever since my husband died I have been feeling more worried about safety at night."

TMI. I'M TELLING strangers "Too Much Information." Some of these conversations may require the "I-just-lost-my-husband" explanation, such as changing the mortgage, but most do not. It was not necessary to tell the electrician that I was now living alone and the person cutting my hair didn't need to see me fight back tears.

Nevertheless, I often describe the dreadful story of my loss. In spite of my early embarrassment over being introduced as a widow, there are other times when I want to tell everyone what has happened to me, to us. Sometimes I keep it to the bare facts, and other times I share too many details and become filled with regret. I keep repeating these varying patterns. Chastising myself is ineffective.

Why am I sharing my distress with strangers? Partly it's because what happened to him, and to us, is at the forefront of my mind. When I see a friendly smile or hear an innocuous "How are you?" I have the urge to announce my reality. The story of his recent death simply jumps to the center of my mind. It pushes aside my other thoughts, and the details spill out of my mouth. I need to tell my story, to recount what happened over and over.

I want sympathy to match how sorry I am feeling for my family and myself. I even want strangers to understand the depth of my grief. I want the world to mourn with me, even though rationally I realize that is not realistic. After all, worse things do happen to other people, and I'm not the only one who has experienced a profound loss. Still I continue to want strangers to acknowledge my loss. I want to hear, "How awful for you and your family."

But I still wonder why am I telling strangers? Why not simply limit my bids for sympathy to my friends and relatives? What is the benefit of a brief comment of support from a person I don't know and will never know? It reminds me of the scripts from television featuring bartenders and taxi drivers. Hairdressers too. We have all seen shows in which the disgruntled boyfriend or newly fired person sits at the bar pouring out his or her woes to a bartender who pours vodka and feigns concern. The bartender, the phone company representative, and the bank teller are safe strangers. With strangers, I have the opportunity to speak without recourse. I don't have to follow-up with more information, I don't have to answer additional questions, and I don't have to see them again. Strangers are a safe outlet, safe recipients for my anguish.

Repeating the story also may be the early start of my lengthy healing process. When people experience traumas, they are often encouraged to review the details of what happened, encouraged to remember and process their ordeal. While the loss of my husband may not be officially recognized as a trauma, it was a personal trauma for me. As I share my recent loss with strangers, I may have the opportunity to work out a small piece of this miserable drama. Sharing bits and pieces of my pain with strangers may help me manage my overwhelming emotions.

What I can do for myself:

I can forgive myself for sharing too much information with strangers. I can tell myself it is not harmful to them, and my disclosure may, in fact, help me get used to the idea of my loss. It may be acceptable to seek sympathy when my loss is so fresh. I expect I will share less with strangers as I come to accept being a widow.

7

Please Invite Me, but Let Me Say No

Family friends suggest I join them to see a movie.

A neighbor organizes a cocktail party.

A close friend invites me to a family dinner.

NICE, CONSIDERATE PEOPLE reach out to me shortly after my loss. And yet, I both crave and dread the invitations. I feel lost and out of control. I'm not ready to go out with a group of people by myself. I'm not ready to acknowledge my sorry state of aloneness. So what do I do? I hesitate, I stammer, I make up excuses. How did a social invitation become a personal burden?

My reality right now is that I just can't decide. One minute I want to go and the next minute I don't. I feel too lonely to stay home alone, but then I might feel even lonelier being with other people when the person I want to be with is no longer an option. I am stuck in my grief.

I just don't know what I want and, more often than not, I am not ready to be sociable and smile, especially in a group setting. It takes effort and energy to be pleasant and then to make small talk. I feel sick inside as I talk about the weather, jobs, and vacation plans. I might go home feeling drained from simple, casual discussions.

It's not that I want to be left alone. That is the last thing I want. I am alone more often than I can stand. I want to be part of a group, a community, and friendships, but sometimes none of these meet my needs. Inside I am screaming, "I want my old life back!" I want that closeness that I can no longer have. I often dislike these well-meant invitations when they highlight what I am missing. I end up avoiding the problem by saying no or backing out of plans I've made. Even activities I used to do can feel wrong, and I am aware of feeling out of place.

I probably sound irritated when people ask me to come over or suggest joining them for a meal. Even the times when I say yes, I am keenly aware of the slightly sour tone that sometimes escapes from me, tainting my acceptance. I find myself feeling guilty and embarrassed as I become aware of my grouchiness, but I am still unable to correct or change my attitude. Others hesitate ever so slightly when I am less than enthusiastic. This, in turn, feeds back on my ambivalence and doubt. I'm aware of the cycle but caught up in it.

I realize other people can't read my mind and do not always know about the debate raging inside me. I realize they just can't tell if I want them to invite me or not. If I were a fly on the wall, I wouldn't know what to think of me either. My refusals are sometimes vague, abrupt, and confusing; my acceptances may be filled with discouragement and sadness. Unintentionally, I may be putting up a barrier and creating the opposite of what I really want.

So I hope others ignore my temporary state of insanity and my ambivalence in response to their invitations. I do want to be asked, I do like to be included, and I am grateful for being considered. So I want other people to keep inviting me, but I also want them to let me say no without repercussions. I am glad they are thinking of me or want to be with me. I need the friendships. I just can't always show it.

What I can do for myself:

I can let those who invite me know how pleased I am for getting their invitation even when I am refusing. I must let them know I'm not ready to venture out but still glad to be asked.

My "no" response is not a "no" to them personally. Our friendship is not on the line, only my own mixed emotions. I can tell them to keep asking, and that in the near future I will start saying "yes." My temporary state of turmoil will surely pass. For now I just need to remember to say, "Thank you."

8

Hug Me

I say goodbye to Meg, and we hug as we part.

I meet Jeannie for lunch, and she gives me a big hello squeeze.

My friend Kendra and her husband Fred both hug me as we meet at the restaurant. I savor these seconds.

WHEN A FRIEND or relative hugs me to say hello or goodbye, I get a strong glimpse of something I am missing. Although I let go, I often have the urge to hang on for dear life. At the immediate moment of the hug, a body ache wells up inside me, distinctly different than the cognitive loneliness I know so well. It is internal and visceral, and it has me thinking about the survival touches that help premature infants to thrive. Hugs seem to replenish my sense of wholeness.

Touch is one of the things that I miss the most after the loss of my husband. I remember too well having someone to sit next to, to lean on, to kiss, and particularly to hug. A touch of the hand, an elbow brushing up against me—these innocuous, unintentional moments of contact were as important as the planned ones. My skin misses the contact that helped me to connect and be part of someone else's life. I yearn for my partner-in-touch.

Of course I took these hugs and unplanned physical contacts for granted. They were part of my life but not always noticed and certainly not really appreciated as they are missed now. When my sensory needs were met, my energy was elsewhere, caught up in my daily life. Now, in contrast, these needs often take center stage. It is when we are missing something that we notice it more.

Now, friendship hugs at greetings and departures have become substitute partner hugs for me, and thus, they are both helpful and horrible. In a helpful way, I can still have a touch-connection, but in a horrible way they naturally fall short. I often remember the special hugs that were just for me and not shared with others. When I used to hug my husband, the meaning hung in the air above us, reminding me that we belonged together.

As I have become aware of my need for contact I have tried to pay more attention to all sensations, especially touch. I snuggle with the dogs and lay down next to them. I scratch them, pet them, and hold them. I know I need them in a way they do not understand, but they enjoy the petting in their own natural way. I spend more time soaking in the sun as I sit outside and let the rays warm me, notice more often the heat of the hot coffee sliding down my throat, more slowly scrunch the soft towels after a shower, and slowly rub extra lotion on my hands. I notice the temperatures, the breezes, and the surfaces in ways I didn't before. I also have increased my awareness of colors, smells, and tastes. It is as if I am saturating my senses to help me cope with my feelings.

I am keenly aware of my senses and their special role in my adjustment. Perhaps my sensory organs are on high alert after this significant loss. They are screaming for attention, and I am scurrying around to make it happen in many small ways. I have become more observant and more mindful. Sensations have moved up the ladder of my awareness and priority.

What I can do for myself:

I can further develop a state of present-oriented mindfulness with regard to the daily sensations and experiences I do have available. I can take more time to observe the greenery around me, eat more chocolate, and splurge to purchase those high-thread-count sheets. I can increase my sensory awareness and nurture it to give caring to myself.

I also have told my close friends how much I appreciate their hugs. The hugs have continued.

9

Inadequate Comparisons of Loss

"I know how you feel. My father died several years ago, and I think about him almost every day."

"My mother felt really sad after my father died too, but she met someone else and remarried a few years later. She seems very happy now. "

"I lost my husband after a car accident about eight years ago. We are in the same boat."

COMPARISONS ARE COMMONLY shared. We want to link with each other so we look for ways we are similar. When one person shares an experience, we search our memory for similar examples. Sometimes we share as a way to create connections that offer support. But often that doesn't work.

I find the comparisons inadequate and somewhat exasperating. When people compare the loss of my husband to the loss of their parent, I feel defensive. Sometimes I stay silent and just listen. When I do this, I feel discouraged inside and I might say to myself "not this one," meaning that this person is now dismissed or checked off my support list. Other times, however, I feel pulled to explain how my loss is different than what they are describing. I may try to convince them that they don't really understand, and when I do this, I worry about undermining the interaction. I fear I sound critical at a time when I am being offered support.

Part of the problem is my age. Most people I know have not lost a spouse, so their association with my grief is their loss of a parent. They share the closest grief experience they have, and to me it is an inadequate comparison.

Other times the loss-in-turn disclosure falls short because other people go on to remember and re-experience their own painful memories. The focus may shift to their story. This cycle can easily happen. When another person shares an event, our own emotions may be primed. We then remember our own situation and may have an urge to share it. Now I do the same thing. When I hear about someone's suffering, the loss of my husband jumps to the surface. Disclosure breeds self-disclosure, and this back and forth flow may lead to unwanted comparisons. When I am on the receiving end of these comparisons, I am left with flooded emotions and unspoken words.

A special set of problems is created with the image of a happy ending with a new relationship and lifestyle. This type of sharing is intended to provide optimism and hope, to reassure me that things will eventually turn out okay. Other people don't want to confront pain-without-hope situations, and so they share the happy ending. Surely they know of unhappy endings as well, but prefer not to accentuate these.

However, my reaction to the prediction of a positive outcome is not positive. I don't like other people anticipating my future and suggesting I can be happy if I just want to. It seems I am being told I have a choice that I'm not sure I really have. Therefore, I feel guilty for my ongoing unhappiness. At the same time, I feel annoyed that the other person has tried to undo my present sadness.

Finally, there are the other widows who share. While their thoughts and feelings may at times provide comfort, other times even these comparisons still seem inadequate. The timing and circumstances of his illness and death are unique in many ways. My thoughts and feelings may also be solely mine. If other widows share with a tentative tone of voice, it often seems helpful. However, when other women "know" how I feel, I bristle.

What I can do for myself:

When people compare my grief with the loss of their parent, I need to step back and realize they are connecting with their own grief experience. I can recognize their intent and welcome their efforts to support me. I might even look for some similarities to foster the bond.

If they have been triggered into a lengthy disclosure of their own, I can let them share and, when they finish, I can take responsibility to continue with my own sharing. I don't have to stop just because they shared as well.

If they are promoting a happy ending to my grief process, I can simply state that I hope I have a favorable future as well. After all, I do hope that is true.

If another widow is sharing and identifying the similarities of our losses, I can appreciate both the similarities and the differences of our experiences and our grief. I don't have to agree with all aspects of the comparison.

10

"At Least You . . ."

"At least you have two great kids."

"At least you had many years together."

"At least you didn't see him suffer too long."

I GRIT MY teeth as I wait to hear what will follow these three words. I brace myself for what is coming next: the "why I should be grateful" mini-lecture. I quickly lost count of the number of times I have heard this bid for appreciation following the death of my husband. I have come to really hate this sentence starter, and I find myself getting angry with the person who has spoken these words.

Let me be clear. I fully recognize my advantages. I know that I've had a great life in so many ways. I am not denying the truth of these ideas.

I am keenly aware that his death could have been worse. It could have happened suddenly with no opportunity to talk. It could have been drawn out for several years. It could have happened when our children were very young.

It's just that hearing this phrase, or the many reasons I should be grateful, does not undo my angst. Certainly, not now.

Timing is one of the main problems with the "at least you" phrase. After just a few months, I remain engulfed in my grief, and I often can't seem to take time out to think at all, let alone consider the positives. I'm just unable to count my blessings right now. I find little room for new thoughts, possibilities, or hypothetical scenarios. I'm caught in the concrete, trapped in the present moment of grief, and anticipating the future. Hearing these optimistic points of view simply adds a measure of guilt to my tears.

I believe that later on I will, in fact, say these "at least you" phrases to myself. When I can think more broadly, I will be able to include this perspective. But again, not now.

In addition to timing, it matters who is saying these words. If in the future these words come from me rather than another person, I may find them helpful. Again, not now, and again, not from someone else.

Of course I have often said these same words to other people. It could, in fact, be helpful for me to consider the positive as well as the negative aspects of this difficult situation. I just can't seem to do it now.

Unfortunately, this "at least you" expression can make me question whether my experience of grief is legitimate. I wonder if there are acceptable levels of sadness according to the type of loss and how much time has passed since it occurred. It's true that my grief could easily be compounded by more adversity.

What I can do for myself:

In my mind I can screen out the "at least you" phrases, bunch them together, and save them for another time. I do not have to buy in to the guilt. I am not an ungrateful person simply because I cannot appreciate the better parts of my life right now.

I can let the pain move through me as I work through my grief, knowing in the future that these perspectives may in fact be useful.

11

The Pain of Mingling

I'M CIRCULATING AMONG a small crowd of people, chatting and saying hello as I usually do at a social gathering. After an hour or so of my conversational efforts, however, I'm tired and ready to be recharged. As if on automatic pilot, I look around for my husband, who often was my charging station. I am struck by his absence, and my fatigue suddenly increases.

I miss having a partner I can safely go back to. Instead I am alone in the sea of faces, trying hard to smile or simply not look out of place. Mingling has become quite miserable to me. The action seems harmless enough, but it is now filled with tension and sadness.

I have to admit that social mingling was never my favorite activity. There is the awkwardness of the time before the event starts or right after it ends, the not-sure-what-to-do moments when your partner is in the restroom or parking the car, the times of strain when you first enter another person's house and the other guests have not yet arrived. Even with ongoing conversations, there may be frequent interruptions as people move from subgroup to subgroup. As I pick up on a new conversation or simply let one go, it helps to have a base of operations, a constant person in the vicinity.

All of these awkward times are worse now. When he and I went to social events together, I had someone I could turn to, a person who would be there in a minute, a partner who knew me well enough to interpret my fleeting eye-roll, someone to understand my avoidance. I could easily tolerate the mingle times when he was there, just knowing I had this attachment.

Although it was easier to mingle as a pair, I attended events on my own, mingled alone, and still managed quite well. Just knowing I could talk to him later or be comforted after returning home was enough to help me get by. The potential for future grounding was all that I needed. I could get support over the phone or through a quick text—just realizing I would be with him later saw me through many uncomfortable situations.

I specifically remember our exchange one evening a year before his illness. I was sitting in a parking lot and called him to share how I wished I could skip a work-related social event. I explained how I didn't really want to go but felt that I should. He listened and then reassuringly said, "You don't have to stay long. Just go in for a few minutes and come on home."

Somehow, his words of encouragement got me out of the car and into the door.

Even comfort-in-imagination saw me through awkward social situations when I had to wait a long time for his actual reassurance. He went hiking or sailing for weeks at a time, and I seemed to tackle these situations without too much tension. I could hear our possible conversations in my head or reassure myself, knowing there was more to me than myself. My identity was plural, and that gave me more inner strength than I realized.

Now that my identity is singular and delayed comfort is no longer available, I have lost courage and stamina. Mingling more often overwhelms me and is increasingly aversive. My previously strong image of support is now hopelessly ineffective. I dislike those few minutes before the program starts or the time standing around during intermission. Temporary lapses of his presence were fine, no problem. But this permanent absence leaves me teetering.

Unfortunately, this increased awkwardness has spread to more benign interactions. Previously, I could be counted on to be where I was supposed to be and to arrive on time. If I said 5 p.m., I'd be there at 5 p.m. But now, I might not leave home until 5 p.m. so I don't have to sit alone waiting or pretending to listen to an important message on my cell phone. Even when meeting just one person, I no longer enjoy the quiet before the other arrives. I have started to dislike the interim times, even when I don't have to mingle. The peace I used to feel in the moments of silence has been replaced by discomfort.

I see myself as a toddler again, only this time without my anchor. Of course we all are essentially toddlers when we face challenges or anxiety-provoking situations; we seek and nurture our relationships to keep us strong and sane. We explore the world and metaphorically run back to "grab the knees" of those we love when the world gives us challenges.

As adults we often have replaced our parents with our partners. These secure attachments invisibly hold us together in the tough times of life. We have all seen how hurt children hold back tears only until their parent returns, or how, as adults, we manage a difficult day at work but later burst forth with complaints when we cross the threshold at home.

So being a widow goes beyond loss and a missing partner. It is also about increased anxiety and confusion due to that missing attachment. It is a new internal instability that requires much more of my energy on a daily basis. As a result I am increasingly fatigued trying to achieve a balanced perspective without a base to hold on to.

What I can do for myself:

I can find new ways to ground myself, using new thoughts and images. I might think of a close friend or picture my children. Perhaps an image of a mountain or stream will provide the peaceful permanence I am looking for. I might even consider what my husband might have said to support me. I can remind myself that I was often delayed in support, yet managed quite well.

12

I'm Boiling Over With Grief

I BOILED OVER this week.

I had a sick feeling throughout my body, my heart raced, and I was no longer hungry. I panicked and obsessively reviewed the details of my loss and my unknown future. When I interacted with other people, I had trouble being present, and I'm sure I appeared distracted. I was preoccupied and not listening well. When I missed what was said, I had to catch up to follow the conversation.

In my mind, I had wandered off. I was remembering the final sequence of his life and wondering if I could have done anything differently. I scanned my memory of the medical appointments, the CT scans, and the fatigue post-chemotherapy. I vividly recalled the last few days. Then I started imagining getting older and being alone. I pictured my inability to manage my own affairs. While married, there would have been two of us joining forces to get by; somehow what one of us could do would surely fill in the gaps for what the other couldn't do. Although I had started the day feeling okay, now I had magnified my anxiety by considering a future with failing health. I was caught in an instant flood of dread, remembering the horrid loss and anticipating the next decades.

I envision my brain as a large pot of water with a lid. The height of the water represents my background level of functioning. As my tension increases, bubbles form, forcing the water inside to rise to the top.

Prior to becoming a widow, the water level was midway up this pot, and the boiling bubbles from stress only rarely went over the top. I was aware of my worries, but they rarely interfered with my daily life.

One of the consequences of becoming a widow is my baseline water level, my background of stress, has risen sharply. I hope this is not permanent. The temperature of the water has increased, the boiling begins more easily, the bubbling steam lasts much longer, and the lid occasionally shoots off. When frustration, fear, or failure hit, there is no longer room for accommodation. Even a slow boil or a quick short boil may result in a spillover that figuratively burns me. Sometimes it burns others too.

In everyday language this means I overreact more often. For example, I heard I needed surgery, jumped ten steps ahead, remembered his many medical appointments, and decided I could not cope with yet another ordeal. It is as if my widowhood disaster left me with less room to cope, ready and on high alert for the next catastrophe around the corner. The internal bar has been raised, and there is less room for rational planning or problem solving.

What I can do for myself:

When this panic occurs, I can close my eyes, breathe deeply, and try to address my vat of boiling water. With the help of my imagination, I can pour some cool water into the container to calm the bubbling. I can picture the thermostat moving down. I can even add ice if necessary, or as a last resort I can secure a tighter lid. I need to do this more often so I can handle bursts of anxiety without the threat of overflow. If these images don't work, I can tell myself, "This phase is not likely to last."

I also can just let myself off the hook. Of course I find stressful events more difficult to manage than before becoming a widow. I expect I will develop better coping strategies over time.

13

I Don't Mind Being a Third, but Not a Fifth, Seventh, or Ninth

I WALK IN and see the empty seats arranged for a holiday dinner. Seven of them. No longer eight. I wait until the couples take their places next to each other. Then I sit. The empty space next to me, the space where he used to be, puts a cloud over my mind.

I am now keenly aware of numbers. I am always noticing and counting. Yes, numbers have an intense meaning for me now that I am a widow. Of course, I am particularly sensitive to not having a partner. The transition from two to one has been much harder than I anticipated. Our world is a world of twos. They are everywhere I turn: at the movies, at lunch, and more and more in the grocery store. I see couples at the park, in the airport, and around my neighborhood. Of course I can't control seeing so many couples everywhere in my daily life. Unless I lock myself up in my house, I will be seeing couples.

But with meal invitations and social events, I can exercise my choice. After this seven-person dinner, I decided to have numbers as one of my guides for couples-based occasions. When I am invited for a meal, I check on the count and make my plans accordingly. Right now I say yes to three but say no—or occasionally say yes and squirm—to thoughts of five, seven, or nine.

So, when friends ask me to an evening with other couples, especially for a sit-down meal, my first question is "How many of us will be there?" I don't want to reply until I hear the numbers. "Oh, it's just us" gives me an instant sigh of relief. I don't always like being a third, but somehow I can manage it. Most of our—now my—friends are couples. How can I be with them without sometimes being a third? I have found I can handle being with just one couple. Somehow I know what to do as a third. I can make conversation, look at both of them at the same time, and not worry that our discussion will subdivide into the two of them speaking with each other while I look on. Somehow it is safe to be a third.

The picture is very different with groups of couples. I find myself on shakier ground. I am more uncertain of the layout of the event or what I might have to face. I have been alone at one end of a table, next to a couple talking only to each other, or otherwise partially removed from the main conversation. I'd like to be confident with couples I know well for, after years of being together, most people are hardly exclusive in their interactions. But with sit-down meals, the missing person next to me is just too obvious.

During these gatherings, I might catch myself saying "we" when I should now be saying "I." I might refer to things my husband and I did together and then perhaps the couples at the table will change the subject to avoid commenting on his absence. Should we all pretend he isn't gone, or should we highlight missing him, wishing he were here? Nobody seems to know how we should act or what we should say. So, mostly we avoid talking about or acknowledging his life or his recent death.

With smaller groups of three, the pretending doesn't happen as often. It might be okay for the three of us to miss him together for a few moments. With just three, it is more acceptable for me to be sad; the avoidance of the missing person isn't as necessary. Even in his absence, in some small way he may be allowed to still be part of this intimate group.

So numbers are important and the count makes a difference, not just to my own social awkwardness but also for the collective awkwardness of a group with a missing member. Perhaps for everyone else too, including a third person is easier to manage than having a fifth, seventh, or ninth in the presence of a missing friend and a new widow.

What I can do for myself:

I suppose I can keep counting until my needs change or my adjustment improves. I don't have to meet anyone else's standards, and socializing can be good, although not a requirement.

Besides noticing the numbers, I can consider the nature of the event. More casual occasions are easier than sit-down dinners with assigned seats. If we are standing and talking while we eat, the division of couples is less salient. Often groups of women will gather and chat together, even at these coupled events. I can choose the types of social occasions I want to attend.

I am learning what I can and cannot handle. I can push myself slightly to move forward, but I don't have to push any harder than I am ready for.

14

The Triggers Surprise Me

LAST WEEK IT was hearing the song "Landslide" by Fleetwood Mac.

While pumping away on the elliptical machine, I was listening to music selections on my phone and humming quietly to some oldies when the trigger hit me. The song started and immediately my eyes filled with tears while my body continued to log the miles—no lag in time, not missing a beat, no thinking required. I could imagine people staring at me, perhaps wondering what was wrong. My embarrassment then replaced my despair.

I was immediately taken back in time; I could picture him sitting on the couch in our TV room, his computer playing our favorite songs from the 70s. We both loved the music from this era. As he called me to come downstairs to join him, the song swept us back to college. He knew I loved that song. I loved him for remembering.

Last month I was triggered while getting ready to walk the dogs. He walked them regularly in the afternoon, and in my mind I can clearly picture him, dog leashes in hand, waving to me as I drove home.

At a party a few weeks ago, it was the dancing that triggered me. As I watched the dancing, I could see his facial expressions and visualize his moves, leaning to his right side as his arms and legs swept forward and back, or holding me close with our hands clasped against his chest. He loved to dance, and we were usually the first ones on the dance floor when the music began.

A few months ago, I missed the touch of his hand on mine as the airplane took off. What will it be next time? Will it be a song or a scene? A touch, a sound, a smell, perhaps a glance, or even an order at a restaurant? I feel surrounded by triggers.

My world is filled with bits and pieces of these reminders, a cacophony of sensory flashes encoded with feelings, ready to fly out without invitation. I imagine they are sitting right at the edge, eager to spring out with just a hint of provocation. Like a screaming baby, they don't care about time or place, only about aiming squarely at me, demanding my attention. They happen automatically as if they had a will of their own.

In response to these unexpected cues, my moods are some-times unpredictable. I can be going along just fine when a trigger grabs me by the throat. I look away to avoid the onslaught. Sometimes I want to tell others what I am remembering, and other times I just will the trigger to go away. I often wish I could quickly fade into the crowd or retreat to being alone.

What I can do for myself:

If I am with others, I can explain my sudden tears so they do not worry about me. I can tell them about the triggers that are often hard to anticipate until they happen. I can tell others, and myself, that my moods will improve. I'm just not sure when.

If I am alone, I can take the time I need to gather my thoughts and feelings.

PART TWO

After a While

THIS NEXT SET of essays was written between several months and approximately one year after the loss of my husband. However, there is no exact time frame or order to these events or my feelings. At the time they were written, I believed I had progressed beyond raw emotions to a phase with a bit more rationality. However, this was not always the case. I continued to find many social interactions to be stressful, and I often felt worse when I returned home after a social engagement.

I could feel the expectations from other people start to change when compared to the time period right after my loss. They were more likely to pose "what" questions, such as "What are you doing this week?" rather than "how" questions, such as "How are you managing?" I started to feel implicit pressure to accept my loss and begin to move on. I wasn't ready to really move on.

As in Part One, I still found it helpful when people suggested definite plans or offered practical help. I was relieved to get an invitation to meet for lunch or suggestions for a hike Saturday morning. I appreciated the folks who realized my ongoing struggle and continued to acknowledge my profound unhappiness.

Some of the themes from this second section are repetitious with those from Part One. I continued to be keenly aware of my loneliness and sensitive to my single status. My grief often bubbled out when I wished it hadn't, and I continued to seek the sympathy of other people. I inwardly bristled at some of the comments I heard and avoided many social opportunities while remaining, nonetheless, unhappy about staying home alone. It is clear I was not always moving forward in my reactions or reflections. Sometimes I took a step backwards, and perhaps more often than not, I was simply writing with a different response to now familiar events or comments.

15

Leaving Without Being Noticed

AS I ENTER the party, I immediately see the couples leaning in towards each other, laughing and smiling. I see only the couples and only the happiness. Somehow I fail to notice the music, the food, and the decorations. The others who may be alone and the couples in the midst of an argument are invisible to me. The happy couples are all I see in my viewfinder. My eyes are focused only on the spaces where I no longer belong.

When I came with my husband, we used to arrive on time, and we didn't rush to leave. At the end of the evening, I would have thanked the hosts and said goodbye before departing. I usually stayed until most people had left. This exit took several minutes, and when I finally left, I felt satisfied and connected with the group.

Before my loss, I did not find social gatherings as tiring as I do now. There were times I left early, but leaving early was legitimate and acceptable. The excuses for going home were usually true: I really did have to get up early the next day.

As I reflect on my current social discomfort, I realize the feelings are not new. In fact, I suddenly remember being thirteen again. I can clearly recall being at a school social and feeling self-conscious as I waited for someone to ask me to dance. I would stand on the sideline, talking non-stop to my best friend to avoid the awkwardness. I would watch the clock waiting for the time to go home. Now, being alone in a crowd is once again a source of insecurity, and, once again, I am trying to find a way to leave.

Without my husband, I no longer have someone to help me plan our exit. There is nobody to say "Let's go." I can't say, "Sorry, he is ready to go." I am my own excuse now.

So, since becoming a widow, I am more likely to arrive late and leave early. I observe the group, watch the couples, try to fit in for a respectable amount of time by smiling and making conversation, and I count the minutes as I figure out how to leave in the smoothest way possible.

When I observe other people getting their coats, relief sweeps over me. The window of opportunity has opened. It is now acceptable to go. When I first became a widow and went to parties alone, I used to leave early but still politely said goodbye—I thought it was the correct way to behave. I thought it would be inappropriate for others to realize I had gone but had not said good night.

But now I've discovered an indirect but self-preserving tactic: I forgo goodbye and thank you, as well as the unnecessary comments and encounters, and I quietly leave without being noticed. I do not provide excuses nobody wants to hear.

I slip out when nobody is looking and worry about explanations later, if asked. I have given myself back some autonomy.

What I can do for myself:

I can avoid self-criticism and accept my "leave quietly" strategy as acceptable, at least for the present. Most of the time, nobody notices my early exits. If they do say something the following day, then I can share my excuses about feeling tired or recovering from a busy week. And, if asked by a close friend, I might even tell the truth, "I still find social gatherings somewhat awkward, but I will hopefully feel more comfortable over time."

If others tell me they are disappointed when I go home early, I will explain my perspective. I can help them to see that I was not being rude, but just self-protective.

16

Returning Home Alone at Night

I JUST WALKED into the house. Luckily the dogs always greet me first, right at the door, jumping and wagging their tails. Not sure what I would do if they weren't there. After petting them, I automatically find the light switch in the kitchen as I have for so many years. The click of the switch breaks the darkness, and I see the dirty dishes in the sink and the papers on the table exactly as I left them. No more and no less mess than when I went out. The stability of the layout disturbs me as a static reminder—nobody else is home to move things around, and nobody is at home to complain about my mess.

It was actually a nice evening but with a difficult and now familiar ending. I met a friend at the theater, and we saw a movie together. For the most part, it was great to go out and take a break. But coming back home is still quite difficult. After the movie, we hugged goodbye in the parking lot, then she left in her car to go home to her family, and I left to drive to an empty house. As I unlocked the door and crossed over the threshold, the facts of my loss announced themselves. In some ways, the nice evening felt ruined.

The downward spiral actually began as I got in my car to drive home. I seemed to be intact until then. I was able to enjoy the movie, the dinner, and our exchange throughout the evening. But driving alone in the dark, even on familiar streets, added to my predictable decline. I might even have hurried a bit, knowing that the sadness was taking over and I hate to drive while feeling so upset. Even more importantly, however, approaching and entering my home, especially in the evening, highlighted my aloneness.

It is odd that leaving the house doesn't seem so bad and does not cause me much turmoil. Kind of amazing to think about the powerful difference between going versus coming. It is the same door, the same sidewalk, the same driveway, and the same time spent alone. Yet the feelings are so very different.

I have a recurring visual image of driving down my dead-end street and seeing his car parked in our driveway. I distinctly remember the relief I would feel when his car came into view. It was a common sequence with consistent physical reactions: put on the blinker, turn the corner, see his car, relax, and breathe more easily. I'd see his car and think in the back of my mind that he was home and everything was in order;

everything was as it should be. I am thankful that I shared this image with him before he was sick, told him how happy I felt when I saw his car sitting in the driveway at home. I always enjoyed our reunions. Now, however, I am driving his car so the usual car does not greet me as I turn the corner to go home. The changed scene is another cue.

Of course, before all this happened, I often went out by myself or with friends without my husband. We both did. It was not unusual. We came and went with ease, coordinating timing and togetherness but not hesitant to have separate experiences. It was an easy flow, and I often think our separate times enhanced the time we spent together—more to share as we experienced the absence but also the reunion. That's it, of course. There was a reunion then, and now that part of the pattern is gone. There is the leaving as before, but no reunion to restore the balance.

With the death of my spouse, these reunions are missing, so the emotional fix for my unresolved issues and the soothing of my pain is no longer available. So, I walk in the door, greet the dogs, and confront my feelings, now without the relief I am looking for.

What I can do for myself:

I can ask others to pick me up sometimes when we go out together, even if it is out of the way. More importantly, I can ask others to come in for a few minutes at the end of evening.

This would help me to fill the house with voices, to ease the adjustment of returning home.

When I must return alone, I can remember to leave more lights on and the radio playing. I need to create a house filled with noise. I also might alter some of the furnishings and put new art on the walls to change some of the familiar cues.

I also can do better planning before I leave. I can intentionally think about something that needs to get done when I get home, such as an email or a phone call. I am not avoiding my grief but managing my grief.

17

Include Me in Your Bad News

"I'm sorry I've been so absent these last few months. A few months before your husband became ill, my mother was diagnosed with Alzheimer's and that has taken up all my energy," says Martha. "I didn't want to give you something else to worry about."

"I haven't called these last few months as I was preoccupied with deciding how to handle my son's school suspension," says Alice.

I HAD NOT considered these reasons for the absence of some of my friends. When people did not call or come by when my husband became ill or after he died, I was filled with disappointment. I wondered if they were avoiding me or too busy to care. I thought perhaps the idea of death was scaring them, or perhaps they felt clueless about knowing what to say at such a difficult time. I just had not thought enough about this other reason: people not calling because they were struggling too. I was caught up in my own feelings of dismay about why Martha and Alice had not been in touch. When I did hear their information, I could have kicked myself.

In my own grief-stricken self-absorption, I had not adequately considered this obvious possibility.

Of course this all makes sense. The world does not revolve around my grief or my loss. I should have considered that there may be difficult and preoccupying situations going on for those I care about. I understand that people can be too overwhelmed to reach out to share their own misery. It is hard enough to live it and, often, even harder to repeat it to an unsuspecting listener. We all have times when we hold our concerns inside to limit the extent we have to face their reflection in the outside world.

People also may feel they should protect those who are already suffering. We do this every day. "I won't tell her about what happened today as she already had a bad day herself." Or "Tell him on the weekend after he's relaxed. His boss really was on his case this week at work." So we may also do this with those who have lost a family member or close friend. We think that we help them to manage by not giving them more to worry about. But is this true?

All these thoughts and this reasoning made more sense to me before the death of my husband. Since my loss, I have had trouble completely accepting this avoidance of sharing bad news. When people don't tell me the news, good or bad, I feel left out of the loop. I want in, even if it's bad news. When I don't know important information or I'm the last one to find out, I feel more isolated from the world around me. My grief feels even larger, as I imagine there is no room to add more problems. I become more limited by my personal frame of mind.

Besides feeling left out, I also wonder if I have let them down. Because I did not know about their difficulties, I was not able to be the caring friend or relative I'd like to be. I was not there for them. Perhaps I would not have done a good job trying to give support to them while I am grieving myself, but some support may be better than none. I would have liked the choice.

I also don't want others to assume I cannot handle more bad news because of my loss. Most of the time now my grief is coming and going, no longer a constant wail as I go in and out of panic and tears. I still do the laundry, get my teeth cleaned, and have the oil changed in my car. I function, even if half-heartedly at times.

I believe we have larger holding tanks than we realize. There is room for our own grief and the grief of others. Attending to other people and thinking about their plight could even be helpful. I know I can actually help myself by finding ways to help others. It can be a relief, a needed break, to step outside my own circumstances and get involved in another person's problems. I can put aside my own thoughts and be there for others.

Of course I don't wish adverse things to happen to my friends and relatives, but when they experience a hard time, I'd like to be told. We then can comfort each other or get through it together.

What I can do for myself:

I can tell other people to share both good and bad news with me. I can let them know that being involved with them helps me stay engaged and avoid isolation. I realize I may not have been a great helper in the midst of my early grief but now as the months pass, I want to step out of my grief to hear more about other people.

I also can continue to ask people about themselves and their lives to be a good friend and to keep the conversations balanced. I will surely get back to my own grief when it hits me again.

18

Hating Weekend Nights and Holidays

Joanne calls me on Monday. "Want to go for a long walk this evening?"

Amie sends me a text on Tuesday. "I have an easy day at work Thursday. Want to meet downtown and have lunch together?"

"Hope you have a good holiday in spite of everything," Tess says when she sees me out walking. "I'll call you after New Year's when my family leaves."

AS A WIDOW, Monday through Friday has suddenly become the better part of my week. Unfortunately, invitations from friends take a dive on the weekends and stop dead in their tracks for Friday or Saturday nights and the major holidays.

I really am grateful for the calls and invitations. It's great when others reach out to me. With my closest friends, I also can push myself to initiate those phone calls or send those texts to create get-togethers. Making and receiving such plans is part of my former repertoire. What has changed is the "when."

As a result of my new status, my own efforts are now boxed in by time. I rarely suggest an activity on a weekend evening with a friend who has a husband or partner. Similarly I avoid seeking contacts during any major holiday. Since becoming a widow, weekends and holidays are quiet. I know people have partners and families, and on weekends and holidays they take time for each other.

Weekend nights, especially Saturday nights, are for couples. Remember when we used to call Saturday night "date night?" My friends with partners make dinner plans and go to movies either by themselves or with other couples. Even after many years of marriage, they need this time to maintain their relationships and to take a break from the hectic workweek. They naturally spend time with their partners as they regroup and unwind. I was part of that same system when my husband was alive. I had a weekday life and a weekend nightlife, organized around being with him or doing things with other couples. One of my favorite things was for us to stay home and do nothing, but that was a "together nothing."

Even though I understand this pattern, I dislike it. It is the weekend nights that I dread the most. I can't help feeling left out by my friends who, naturally, block me out on the weekends and pop me back in during the week. It may not be convenient to see me on a weekend night, but don't they get it? Being a widow is not convenient for me either. Don't they know I have nothing to do?

I am not surprised to be lonely on the holidays. Being a new widow means celebrating holidays, often alone, without my husband. My children are grown, live out of town, and won't always be spending every holiday with me. This part of it I get. Of course I don't like it, but I'm trying to accept it.

Sometimes other people even avoid inquiring about my holiday or weekend plans. They might feel uncomfortable if they hear I have nothing to do, so they simply do not broach the question.

Similarly, people may be reluctant to mention their own future plans. They are off to a brunch or a party and leave it out of what they share. If I don't ask what they are doing, they may keep it to themselves. I can sense the active withholding of information, and this makes me uncomfortable. Of course I know they have activities planned, and I am keenly aware that they are not sharing them with me. It somehow just makes for an uneasy exchange.

Of course, I must be honest. It is true that sometimes I *would* prefer they not share too many details about their weekends and holidays. At the same time, however, I would rather feel sad and envious than experience the tension of obviously withheld information. When there is an awkward pause in the conversation, I fill in the gap with my mind. If I ask, "What are you doing this holiday?" and other people hesitate, I imagine the greatest of plans. So, I would rather hear briefly about the festivities and let myself feel sad, than wonder what they really are doing that they don't tell me.

None of this surprises me. As soon as he died, I knew weekends would be the worst part of the week. I can forget and distract myself with the structure of work and daily routines. But my former weekend routine was my people routine, a family and partner routine for me too. Even after my empty nest began, weekends stayed special, changing from family time to couple time.

I realize I was lucky to have many years with my husband and family. Now, in many ways I feel back at square one before marriage. I find myself thinking of the specialness of the weekend. Sometimes I get bogged down and moody as I look at my friends with their partners. I feel dejected when my phone doesn't ring on the weekends or I realize that I have no place to go on a holiday.

I realize this complaint cannot be resolved, and I also know that sometimes I whine about it. A loss is a loss, and I certainly don't believe my life could be the way it was when he was here. I don't really expect coupled friends to always call me or to spend time with me when they have their own families. But I am still raw and depressed, and I notice weekend nights and holidays in a way I never did before.

What I can do for myself:

First, I can try to think of my weekends and holidays as important times for my feelings and thoughts. I can spend time journaling on my computer, feeling sad or reminiscing, just letting myself be. I can use this special time for these self-reflections.

I can try to make other plans during these family-based times. If I am hesitant to attempt planning with others, I can focus on household projects, such as painting a room or organizing my papers. I can watch a movie I have longed to rent or read a book that has sat too long on my shelf. I can take my weekly trips to the grocery store, recognizing with gratitude that nowadays stores are no longer closed on weekend nights. I've started working out on Saturday nights when the gym is open. I have volunteered at a shelter and played catch up with email communications. I try to think about all of the times in the past when I've complained about being too busy and not having time to myself.

I also want to remind myself that not hearing from friends during these times is not an intentional exclusion. I remember being so busy preparing for a gathering that I probably missed people who did not have plans. Since almost all my friends are couples, they, like me, are not used to having an unattached friend who might be alone.

I also could contact acquaintances that I know are alone like me. But these comrades of the single life are not close friends yet, and that takes time to develop. I need to encourage myself to be patient, take more risks to get to know new people, and realize that some of these new friends may become close friends.

I know in time I will get better at managing holidays and weekend nights.

19

Sharing My Widowhood Too Soon

"I lost my husband last winter."

I WAS MILLING around at a cocktail party when it slipped out. I wished I hadn't said it the minute the words left my mouth. Such a statement clearly stops conversation in its tracks. The flow of conversation is disrupted and only one direction is acceptable: "I'm so sorry to hear that," says the recipient of this blunt admission. Silence or strain then follows. Subsequently, it is up to me to rescue the exchange and change the topic.

I didn't know anyone other than the hosts, and as I walked up the sidewalk, I felt anxious but resolved to push myself to attend this gathering. When I opened the door, I realized I wasn't prepared for the "getting to know you" scenario. With strangers, it always starts in the same way. We share how each of us knows the host and then our personal demographics, including where we live, how many children we have, perhaps trips we have taken, and of course, the kind of work each of us and our spouses do. This used to be the easy part of any introduction for, after all, I knew all the answers. There was not much to think about, and the responses were routine.

But now these simple questions fill me with apprehension. How do I answer the partner portion of the conversation? Share it or bypass it? What are my options?

I can do what I did tonight when the words rushed out of me. I said the truth about my loss. However, sharing intense information too early in the conversation is not a good idea. It is a showstopper, and it can channel the attention entirely to me if I am not mindful to turn things around. I quickly brought up something else but the damage was done. I erred by sharing something too emotional too early.

So after this too-early-telling I tried the other option for the remainder of the evening. With the rest of the people I met, I said nothing about my living situation or my spouse and stayed on the safe topics of work, books I enjoyed, and the recent bad weather. I simply bypassed any spouse questions. This seemed to go smoothly, although it did not feel right. I felt like I was holding back. I was not really going to get to know them, and they certainly were not really going to get to know me. There are no real guidelines on how or what to share.

I now recognize my own biases when I think about what and when to disclose to new people. I really enjoyed being married, not only for the daily partnership but also for how I felt more complete as a married person. I wish my marital status did not directly impact my self-esteem as much as it does. When my husband died, I lost part of my sense of self.

What I can do for myself:

If I can't share my widowhood and I can't comfortably be silent, what are my options when I meet new people? There has to be something in between. There always is.

I imagine the key is to wait and share. I don't want my being a widow to be the first thing others learn about me, but I don't need it to be the last either. I can share the easy demographic information first, get to know them, and see if a connection develops. After more time, in-depth conversations may ensue and then I can share my loss. In this way people will get to know me, a person who is experiencing grief, rather than only the grief itself. I am learning the when and how of sharing about my loss.

20

Talking to the Dogs

"Okay, first we are going to have supper, then we'll go for a walk."

"Let's go downstairs and watch some TV to relax."

"Come here, and I'll brush you."

THESE ONE-WAY CONVERSATIONS take place at home with my dogs. Since losing my husband, they have become the de-facto beneficiaries of my need to talk when I'm alone. I imagine my conversation with the dogs has at least doubled since becoming a widow. I'm sure the amount of time I spend thinking about them and considering their needs has doubled as well. They have gained from my loss.

Is this a good thing? Perhaps yes, perhaps no. On the positive side, I am glad to have living beings in my house. I think they have literally kept me sane, and they are an important buffer against the silence of being alone. At least I'm not always talking to the walls, although sometimes I do that too. They never cease to welcome me, and they definitely ease the transition from the outside world back to my home. If I drift off into self-pity, they invariably pull me back to everyday life with their insistence to eat or to go outside. I imagine widows with children at home find the demands of their children sidetrack some of the time for personal sorrow.

My dogs also provide a target for my attention. I can pet them and scratch them while they listen to the details of my day. In these ways, they meet a small bit of my need for contact and interaction. In the middle of the night or at odd hours, my dogs are always available when my friends are not. They represent consistency and security.

My dogs also increase my options for activities when my friends are all busy. I can almost always go to the dog park and find other folks milling around in this social situation with relaxed demands. I walk them each day, both for their sake and my own. It was my husband's job to walk the dogs each day, so after his death, I found this task burdensome. Very soon, however, I realized our walks were a good addition to both the structure of my day and my physical health.

On the pessimistic side of my post-loss dog focus, I wonder about the impact of my increased attachment to them. When I'm out of the house for a long period of time, I think about them more than I did before. I am worried the dogs are now taking up too much of my energy. Channeling too many of my internal resources towards them may further deplete my limited stamina.

I have had two dogs for many years. I lost my older dog a few months after I became a widow. I hardly remember her death as I was still in shock over the loss of my husband. Not surprisingly I soon found another rescue dog and continued my two-dog household. Husbands cannot be replaced, so this contrast adds to my sadness.

More recently, I remembered the death of this older dog and have regretted the matter-of-fact way I quickly buried her ashes in the backyard. I find myself thinking about her now and providing some space for this additional unhappiness. As I recognize this secondary loss, I have started anticipating the death of my next dog. Being a widow has intensified my awareness of past and future losses.

I ask myself if my increased interest in my dogs contributes to my avoidance of other opportunities. Should I meet a friend for dinner or hurry home to feed the dogs? It is very hard to tell if I'm avoiding, simply coping, or taking care of two dogs as a single person.

At home, the tone and substance of the one-way conversations are totally in my control. In contrast, socializing with people usually requires a modicum of enthusiasm. When talking to the dogs, I have exclusive say-so to determine the amount of talk, the tone, and, of course, the topic. I always get the last word.

What I can do for myself:

I have made myself aware of this issue and can now monitor myself a little more carefully to ensure balance. It is fine to spend more time and energy with the dogs, as long as I am continuing to encourage myself to stay involved with other people.

21

Will Other Single People Be There?

"Hey, want to come for dinner Saturday evening?" Beth says with a wide smile. "We're having some folks over and would love for you to join us."

I pause briefly and then ask, "Will other single people be there?"

I ASK THIS awkward question too quickly. When she replies yes, I am more likely to respond yes. If the answer is no, my go-to response is to explain that I can't make it or, if I know the person very well, I might say I'm still not ready to handle this yet.

In addition to checking on the number of guests, I now ask if others, besides me, are coming alone. This question of how many singles has become another sorting strategy for social invitations. I've learned my lesson after feeling fairly miserable at too many couples-only events. Now if I hear everyone else is a couple, I have learned to say no. If other people are coming alone, *then* I decide if I want to go. It is unfortunate that these social occasions that I used to relish continue to be fraught with awkwardness and anxiety.

The pain behind my question is intense. Asking this question is an instant pathway to my grief. I feel a cloud coming over me, and my stomach tightens. I steel myself inside. I strain to stop the rush of feelings that are right below the surface. Someone kindly invited me over, and I probably look like I just heard bad news.

I hate questioning this way, and I dislike my hesitancy. It seems rude to question the nature of the group before I respond; it's like asking what food will be served when receiving a dinner invitation. I really try to show a pleased face when an invitation comes my way, but somehow I doubt I really pull it off. I know people must see me flounder as I ask one of my "flip of the coin" questions. After hearing my concern, others may wish they had not invited me. The hosts should not have to evaluate the group composition on my behalf.

This now routine question highlights how out of place I continue to feel in social situations. It is hard for me to relax with a group, hard to be myself, hard to be *by* myself.

Since becoming a widow I remain in unchartered territory. I want to stay connected—I need to stay connected—but I don't always know how. I can't be like I used to be, but I don't know how to be now. I need a new script and then I require lots of practice. But the scripts keep changing as I move from feeling sorry for myself to pushing myself to forge ahead. One minute I think, "I can do this," and the next minute I am asking myself, "Are you kidding?"

Even with a favorable response to my question—"Yes, there will be others coming by themselves"—I still can't completely relax. I move on to a new round of doubt and anticipated awkwardness. Perhaps the other singles are younger than I am or simply people coming to the party without their partners. What if the other singles don't show up? I find myself anticipating the subgroups that naturally develop, wondering which one I can join when I get there. I must be in a theatrical role I don't feel suited for. I don't want to say yes to something I won't enjoy.

Of course all of this worry often backfires on me even when I assume that other folks are coming on their own. Because of my doubts, I have to push myself even harder to walk into the party, smile, and interact. I spend too much energy planning to manage something intended to be fun. But staying home is just not the answer all the time. It is clear to me that the problem is not really managing myself in a group but rather managing the new version of myself in a group.

What I can do for myself:

I can accept that these decision-making steps are part of my new social process. I can smooth over the situation by simply inquiring about who is coming and then say I'll check if the date works for me. That way I am not responding immediately. The "I'll check and call you tomorrow" approach is frequently used in the work environment and is often quite effective to organize time and obligations in a socially acceptable manner. It probably will serve me well now for social invitations.

22

Being Second Choice

"My husband's out of town. Want to get together this weekend?"

I HEAR, BUT also keenly *feel* these introductory words. Too many times the social invitation, particularly if it's for a rare weekend plan, begins with this phrase. A friendly offer, a simple suggestion, now stings with an out-of-proportion intensity. Truly, I am glad to be called, yet overly aware of the disclaimer.

I know I am rarely anyone's first choice, and this makes sense to me. Before becoming a widow, I too considered even close friends as a second choice much of the time. I'm sure I used this disclaimer myself, but with other married friends it was acceptable and even assumed.

Of course it would be strange if a married friend always called me first. I would start to worry: Is her relationship faltering? Is she concentrating too much on me? No, it's not a frequent invitation that I am looking for; it's just that this sentence, "He's out of town, so I am free" triggers memories and underscores my pain. It reminds me of how couples usually organize their time, or at least how we used to juggle ours.

I miss how my husband and I regularly discussed our schedules and knew what the other one had planned. We even had a weekly coordination meeting that we called "calendars." This time was particularly critical while our children were growing up, and included items like who's picking up whom, and who's doing what for each child each day. But even after the kids left home, we continued to communicate, to be aware of what each other was doing. That negotiation is now gone. I have nobody to show my schedule to and nobody to work my schedule around. Instead I wait for other people to make their arrangements, for their plans to shake out, and I fit in where I can. I miss both the hassle and pleasure of coordinating.

I don't say any of this out loud. I keep it to myself and try to tell my distressed insides to let it go. Nobody said I had to be first; it's not my right or privilege to be first. But this phrase makes it clear that what I am missing is a priority person.

What I can do for myself:

I need to accept this phrase and not attach so much meaning to it. I realize my sensitivity antennae are still set too high. I'm almost looking for reasons to feel sadder, but I don't need an excuse for my grief.

I don't have to apply an all-or-nothing rule with others. It isn't "number one or bust." There are many types of friends, and friends have always been special in ways husbands are not. I continue to have friends and relatives at different levels of closeness and can enjoy even those who are not my best friends.

When I am feeling sorry for myself about being second, I can remember my own previous patterns. I used to use this phrase without thinking of its impact. I called people at the last minute when my husband was out of town or initiated an evening get together when he went to bed early. I announced that he was gone for the weekend and I was ready to get together.

I hope in the future that I learn to appreciate the freedom that being single can bring. I have glimmers of this advantage. Every once in a while I notice that I can be more spontaneous. I can say yes without checking.

23

Missing Out on Activities

"There's a series of concerts playing at the botanical garden!" my friend Allison mentions enthusiastically. "I'll talk to Fred tonight about getting some tickets for us."

"A new restaurant opened up in midtown. We can't wait to try it this weekend," says Lisa.

WELL, THE "US" and the "we" in these conversations are not directed at me. It is not a "please join us" invitation.

This used to be me. I'd see something I wanted to do and, most often, could suggest or even convince my husband to go to a concert, an art festival, and even sometimes to a museum exhibit. Sometimes I'd see if he wanted to have others join us; sometimes we'd go alone. I had these choices, and when plan A did not happen, I had plan B to fall back on. I'd find a way to make the activity happen if it was something I really wanted to do.

Now my ideas fall flat, and my choices are limited. When I hear about a movie I really want to see I quickly think, *Ugh, I must either go alone or try to find someone to see it with.* The former option is not often appealing and the latter option can be just too much work.

Finding a way to attend an event with another person is not an easy undertaking, yet I still seek companionship to see the art exhibit or hear the concert. But now there are procedures to consider in order to recruit friends to join me. Most often, I just tell myself not to bother, and I miss out on movies, shows, or exhibits I'd really like to see. I had automatic ready access with my willing-to-tag-along spouse.

Yes, I could learn to do more things alone, and I am doing more things by myself by necessity. I just spent three days alone in a new city and found the adventure limited and rather disappointing. The enjoyment was not the same. When there is nobody to say, "Look at that!" or nobody to whom I can say, "Let's go try that!" I do not enjoy myself as much. So the issue is not my ability to go alone, it's my willingness and my personal preferences.

I used to believe that the activity was secondary and the person I went with was primary. That way if the activity was less than exciting or entertaining, we both still won. We could both complain about the food, the weather, or the play. We were comrades in disappointments and in delights. Now, that order of priorities no longer seems to hold. When I see an activity that interests me, I *then* have to search, ask, and plan. It feels topsy-turvy; first, I must identify the activity and then find the company. I dislike this sequence, the time it takes, the arrangements it requires, and the reminder that my permanent partner is missing. My first choice option is gone.

What I can do for myself:

It probably comes down to conserving my resources. I have to be more selective when choosing activities for which I would like a companion. That way I won't be tired from the process or putting too much energy into the less-desirable options. I will participate in fewer activities but do not have to give them all up.

I also can join existing groups so the activities are not mine to organize. Although I would prefer being with just one or two people, I need to get more comfortable with groups. The only way I know to get more comfortable with groups is to join them. I can go to outdoor activity groups, social meet-up groups, a lecture at the university, or a professional workshop where couples and partners are not usually present. In these settings, people are usually going to the event by themselves, even if not when they return home. These group activities are becoming more of my focus to keep me out of the find-a-companion sequence.

24

Remember Me on His Birthday

"This is the hospice calling to check in. We know it is your late husband's birthday this week."

TEN MONTHS AFTER my loss, I was surprised to receive a call from the hospice organization that helped us in the last few days of his life. They were calling just for one reason: they knew, or had at least recorded, his birthday and asked how I was doing with this upcoming date. I was grateful to have them acknowledge his birthday, this particularly painful date for me.

In addition to the anniversary of the day of his death and our wedding anniversary, his birthday is clearly a time of increased emotion.

When we think of a birth date, we think of life, and when we think of life's journey, we come to death. These dates are inextricably linked, and thinking of one end of the spectrum naturally highlights the other. Yet, except for my immediate family, people in my life probably do not remember, or maybe never knew, his birthday. They are more likely to recall the time of year when he died but will not think to inquire about the day he was born. Were it not for Facebook reminders of his upcoming birthday and the request to write on his timeline, even some relatives might forget when his birthday comes around.

And yet, I cannot and do not forget when he was born. It isn't just the date that's important. It is marking his time and the era of his life. If he had not been born when he was, we would not have met, and we would not have fallen in love, married, and had a family. Even if the day of his birth was changed by just a few years, we may have missed our first interaction. Perhaps we would not have met that serendipitous day on a Sierra Club hike.

Time and timing are the critical creators of everyone's relationships and lives. I am forever in time's debt.

However, beyond the philosophical musings about time and the mystery of unexpected contacts, there is the yearly expression of special reminders. Years are marked by what we did on a birthday, how we spent a summer, where we were watching fireworks on the fourth of July. As his birthday approaches this year, the cruelty and the joys of birthday reminders are embedded in my mind.

I remember the celebrations we had over the years, the successful and not-so-successful gifts, and all those birthday poems I wrote. I remember the birthday hunts around the house reflecting our family tradition of hiding gifts in grocery bags and writing clues for finding each gift. Even our family dog went prancing around the house with us as a pack of gum was found in the microwave or a new CD was hiding in the shower. Birthdays were for candles, cake, playfulness, and family wholeness.

These joyful birthday memories are now replaced with emptiness. Celebrations for him are gone and even the days leading up to his special day are filled with gloom. While I can give up the games, the gift hunt, and the rhyming poems, it seems impossible to process missing him on his birthday. I think of the birthdays we will never share and wonder how to best mark this day that remains special for him and for me.

I believe birthdays are more personal than other holidays and so perhaps more important. While holidays are for everyone, birthdays are for one person at a time. The birthday person becomes the center of attention for one day. For those celebrating, they focus their energy on the beloved family member or friend by honoring him or her with gifts and closeness.

So on his birthday, his missing person cannot be replaced. There is no substitute person to receive my attention. In my world, nobody else lays claim to the day. All I can do is remember him and the birthdays of the past. To help his birthday continue to be important, I want others to share in these memories, but also to remember me remembering him.

What I can do for myself:

On a personal level, I can prepare for these important days. I can do something special in his memory such as plant a tree, make a donation, or write down some memories of birthdays past.

With others, I can let them know that this day will be difficult for me. It is important to let them know before the date arrives. I cannot assume others will remember, but I can ask them to join me in recalling him on his birthday.

25

"You Must Be Feeling Better"

"Last weekend I went on a hike along the Chattahoochee with a local outdoor club," I share with my co-worker. "It was really hot, but it felt good to be along the water exercising."

"Great! You've joined a hiking club," Janice says, smiling. "So glad you are getting out. You must be feeling better."

I ONLY WISH this were true more of the time. Other widows have shared similar experiences of becoming dismayed when hearing, "You must be feeling better" when they went shopping, had their hair done, took a Saturday road trip, or bought a new car. Other people jump on these events as signs of improvement and resolved sorrow. They are keen to have us quickly return to pre-grief life. But I'm not ready for my grief to be completely gone. Sometimes, I feel rushed to be more okay than I feel.

Compared to my pre-widowed self, a large part of me continues to feel quite vulnerable. I still cry sometimes when I see his name on the mail or find an old mother's day card. I find the late hours of the evening and the early morning filled with bits of dread. Seeing old family pictures or cleaning out old papers remains grueling. My adaptation to this loss is uneven, even with the new activities I've taken on.

As the months have passed, I have become better at keeping my chronic sadness out of the conversation, and I'm sure that makes me appear stronger than I feel.

Of course there is truth in their statements about my progress and steps for recovery. That is probably why I feel defensive. I am certainly managing better, especially compared to the months right after my loss. I venture out more and try new things. I make more plans and say yes more often. Although I think about him much of the time, there are more and more hours when I am thinking about something else.

However, my new activities do not necessarily equate with full recovery. My momentum has indeed improved, but my emotions often lag behind, and profound anguish can return suddenly with a vengeance.

In spite of my steps moving forward, I still appreciate being asked about how I am *really* managing his death. I am glad when others do not assume I'm completely recovered and don't take "fine" for an answer simply because I joined a new club or made a new friend or because more time has passed. My outer persona is doing better, while my inner self still lags behind much of the time.

What I can do for myself:

I can acknowledge to myself that indeed I am doing better even if I'm not "over it." When another person comments only on the favorable adjustments I have made, I can just let it go. I do not need to restate the negatives.

I realize that not everyone assumes I am back to "normal," and many accept my ongoing sadness.

I find others are more receptive when I share my progress first before sharing any darker thoughts. By sharing both the plusses and minuses of my journey, I acknowledge my improvements in the context of my ongoing pain.

26

My Closest Friends Get the Worst of Me

"How are you doing?" "Okay. Thanks for asking."

"How are you doing?" "Up and down. Some days are harder than others."

"How are you doing?" "Still often depressed. Hard to believe it's been so long since he died. I still feel overwhelmed and . . ."

SAME QUESTION, DIFFERENT responses from me. It all depends on who is doing the asking. In the first interaction, I am speaking with a casual acquaintance. In the second interaction, I'm speaking to a good friend from college who lives in another state. In the third interaction, I'm sitting with a close friend with whom I can speak openly.

These levels of sharing require monitoring on my part. I am operating with two trains of thought. There is the part of me that remains ready to burst forth with how awful I feel and a second part that is watching how much I disclose depending on my relationship with the other person. This dual processing makes me tired.

I try to consider my audience when discussing my thoughts and feelings. Of course I am more honest with the people I know best. This works well most of the time. Disclosing more details of my personal life helps me feel closer and encourages them to share in turn. I relish the exchange and the bond that only true sharing brings.

When talking about negative events, the outcome varies depending on the intensity and duration of the topic. If it is a flat tire, a disappointing day, or how I lost money as a vulnerable consumer, I can be furious and still maintain a healthy exchange with my friends. Because the topics are short-lived, I can even throw in some humor, and we can commiserate together about the vagaries of life. We complain back and forth and enjoy the exchange in spite of undesirable content. Even with more serious or ongoing stressors, sharing continues to encourage good feelings between us.

With this loss of my husband, however, I remain in uncharted territory due to the chronic, unending nature of my problem. I cannot always find a safe or middle ground for sharing. I often end up at extremes, either saying nothing or going too far and spewing my inner misery. The people I really care about endure my brutal honesty and my deep despair. They get the real me, but it happens to be the worst version of me. I'm not sure how I manage to censor myself with acquaintances, but somehow access to my true self remains closed off. It is the same coping I use for work or to get through day-to-day life. With someone I am closer to, I can't seem to find the shut-off valve.

When I try to alter this undesirable discrepancy, I am not very successful. I will literally tell myself to say "fine" or instruct myself to keep my mouth quiet when a good friend asks me how I am coping. I try really hard not to reveal too much of my distressing outlook with my immediate circle. When I invariably fail to keep the gloominess out of my words, I go to plan B and try to cut my sentences short. That hasn't worked too well either.

Sometimes I step back and think about this unfortunate pattern. I wish I could reverse the pattern—share my frantic sadness with casual friends and mention more happiness with those I care most about. Of course, I couldn't really share the grief-stricken side of me with casual friends or acquaintances, as that may curtail the developing relationship. However, I hate that I end up sharing the majority of my misery with just a few friends. I don't do a good job of spreading out my grief.

What I can do for myself:

The only thing I've come up with is to discuss my awareness and regrets about this pattern. I can tell my closest friends that I realize it is unfair that they see me at my worst.

More recently, I've noticed some improvements in my monitoring success, and I've become more adept at sharing selectively, but this process is much slower than I thought it would be. Eventually, I will get even better at keeping a lid on my emotional feelings, and I know at some point I will need to disclose much less. I am surprised at how difficult it is to hold back with someone I am close to. I do not handle this aspect of being a widow nearly as well as I thought I would or think I should.

27

"Wasn't That a Great Party?"

"It was great to see you last weekend. We had so much fun Saturday night!"

I AM NEVER sure how to respond at this point. I have several options, none of which provides satisfaction and all of which leave me feeling slightly estranged.

Sometimes I simply agree with the other person and just go along with a positive, albeit not completely truthful, account of the evening. This is probably the easiest option. I don't make waves, and nobody is uncomfortable around me. Of course this remains a little tricky for me to do. I never was good at phoniness.

At other times, especially when I'm feeling sorry for myself, I counter this enthusiasm with a reminder that dancing, drinking, and laughing at a party without a partner is still lonely for me.

Other people usually respond in two ways: either they change the subject, or they restate the more favorable memories of the evening, as if to convince me.

If they choose to change the subject, my experience has been bypassed, although I completely understand that they are not interested in a downwardly spiraling conversation and would like to avoid heaviness at this time. I feel somewhat ashamed of ruining their good memories. They are happily recounting our recent social event while I'm countering them and disrupting the flow of the story. They are not looking for in-depth analysis when they are simply reviewing the events of a previous weekend. They do not want to hear that something they enjoyed produced unhappiness for me. They may know this is true, but again, they don't want to hear it.

If they choose to subsequently restate or elaborate on the positive view of the party, I also feel badly. I know they did not listen or did not want to hear my point of view. They try to sway the conversation to be more upbeat by restating the fun they had, trying to get my complaints to go away or slip quietly into the background.

Either way I feel in a bind. I can't agree, and I can't counter as both have awkward outcomes for me. Therefore, of late I have tried the middle ground, saying something like, "I really enjoyed X but still felt badly about Y." While this may be a more accurate and certainly a more balanced statement, I still may experience a certain amount of social awkwardness. I have taken the good aspects of the evening, and I have added spoils. Other people don't want a tarnished piece of silver or a dress with a stain. Understandably, they prefer to simply enjoy reviewing an enjoyable social event.

What I can do for myself:

At this point in time, I need to accept that most people do not want me to share my heartache anymore. They can't really understand that I am still feeling lost, and if they do, this makes them uncomfortable. They want to enjoy themselves and are less interested in hearing the limits of my pleasure.

They probably are correct. I need to stop sharing my grief unless I am directly asked. In this way, I can ensure my friendships do not take a dip, and truthfully, this sharing is probably no longer helping me either. I therefore must stay neutral until I'm ready to be more upbeat. I can try to keep my attention on the other person's experience.

If I really need to express a negative reaction, I can write down my feelings or call another widow. She almost always understands the limitless outlook of my social pain.

28

"When Are You Going to Start Dating?"

Teresa says with an expectant grin, "So, when are you going to start dating?"

Jo asks, "Would you consider getting married again?"

Amy states, "You know Pat met her new partner online."

MY MOUTH IS open, but I say nothing.

These questions and statements implying I should date were asked sooner and more often than I was ready for. They started less than a year after he died, long before I even considered this option. At first I simply became angry as I pictured an inadequate replacement. I thought my friends were moving far ahead of me and that they were presumptuous to even ask me about dating. I believed they were minimizing my loss and clearly did not understand the anguish I continued to experience. I hated their suggestion that I might move on.

Now, as time continues to pass, my mindset is different, and my reactions to these same questions are changing. I am not always silent. I wonder out loud if I should, could, or want to, as I share my mixed feelings with my friends and colleagues. However, while I have started to consider the topic of dating, loneliness clouds my judgment and limits my perceived options. Loneliness both propels me to consider trying to meet new men and, at the same time, stops me from being a confident seeker.

So when asked these questions now, my ambivalence rears its head. I feel confused, and my responses are all over the place depending on my frame of mind. I have responded defensively, with annoyance, and with yearning, all varying with the day and my mood. I don't like being alone, but I am not sure if I should fix the situation by looking for a partner or whether adapting to singlehood is a better, or certainly more feasible, option.

If I follow the "looking for partner" stance, what does that mean for me? I have not gone on a date in over thirty years. I would become a teenager again with the accompanying doubts and anxieties. I don't know the protocols or how to manage the websites. I don't have enough practice with rejection that I surely will face. I don't even know who I'm looking for. Lots of unknowns. If I forge ahead, it is risky and potentially very discouraging.

At the same time, I realize looking for a partner or even just a companion is potentially a good thing. I found it really helpful to read about other people having new relationships. Meeting someone new would not erase my marriage or the many good years we shared. It would be part of a new phase of my life.

Whether I choose not to look, or if I look and do not find, I need to revamp my view of being alone. I need to change my attitude about being a widow. I can no longer see being on my own as such an undesirable option. I need to embrace this unplanned change and become more comfortable going places by myself so my activities are not so limited. I need to make better use of my time alone so I feel satisfied instead of frustrated and lonely.

What I can do for myself:

I can spend more time considering whether or not to pursue dating. It may be best to make a sequential decision, deciding for the next three- to six-months, and then deciding again. I can change my goals as I continue to experience shifts of attitude as time passes.

I can explain my approach to my well-meaning friends by sharing short-term decisions rather than long-term goals. I may start dating, hate it, and turn away from it, or I may decide to delay and reconsider later on. Regardless of the path I choose or the ultimate outcome, it will help if I rethink my view of being single as an opportunity for new adventures, whether shared or not.

29

The Guest Option in Formal Invitations

IT ARRIVED IN a beautiful envelope with my name and address written in calligraphy. Nowadays, only my name is on the outside. This fact remains upsetting. The dual-to-single reduction of names on the envelope is a repetitive reminder of my loss. While I am getting used to finding household bills addressed only to me, somehow a special invitation is harder to receive when it would have been addressed to us both.

As this is my first post-widowhood formal invitation, I am on guard. Will the inner envelope include "and guest" or will my name alone be listed? Will the response card itself have a space for number attending, or will there only be room for me to respond yea or nay? Either way I lose.

Probably a wedding invitation, I assumed, or perhaps a milestone birthday or retirement occasion. Without even thinking about it, I quickly opened the envelope to check the invitation inside—searching for the occasion and, more importantly, searching to see how the guest option was handled. Even happy invitations now pose a problem.

If it says "bring a guest," I am aggravated and stressed at the same time. The nerve of the hosts to suggest I find a date. Do they think I can just conjure one up on demand? Do they know the pressure this short phrase produces?

What if I accept the guest option? Who qualifies as my guest? Can I bring a friend who is willing to come, or can I get one of my adult children to agree to accompany me? With this debate about "if" and "who," I move from anger to distress. I don't really have anyone to bring. I don't know the rules of etiquette regarding who is an acceptable guest. These questions are new to me.

However, the alternative, the no-guest option, brings little relief. If the invitation did not suggest bringing a guest, if my name alone is on both the invitation and response card, I experience the same mixed feelings—this time, however, after a brief period of relief. After realizing I do not need to rack my brain to think about a suitable guest, I move to annoyance. I imagine that others know I don't have a guest to bring, and then I get sad again as I remind myself they are right—no guest is available or ready to come.

My worry about the guest option soon accentuates my dread at the idea of being present at a large social event alone. As soon as I post the invitation on the refrigerator, I cannot get this anxiety out of my mind. I know I will have to dress up, arrive alone, search for a friend to talk to, decide where to sit, and brace myself to survive several hours with a smile on my face. While I really do want to support the new retiree, the married couple, or the parents-to-be, it is hard not to turn selfishly inward and become focused on my own loneliness.

Formal invitations cannot correctly manage the guest option because there *is* no acceptable option. There is no way of inviting me without triggering my tense reactions, in spite of my excitement for the occasion itself.

Of course this is not a situation that's unique to me. Whenever a person is alone and invited to a momentous social occasion, the people sending the invitation consider whether to say "and guest" or not. Similarly, the single recipient may experience tension regardless of the inclusion or lack of the phrase. Both options present a problem; both may feel like salt rubbed into a wound.

My anger and sadness, unfortunately, get merged with someone else's joyous event.

What I can do for myself:

I can recognize the lose-lose options here and see beyond my own situation. Occasions are not created for, nor are they reactions to, my personal dilemma. I want to focus on the real reason the event is happening: someone is graduating, getting married, retiring, or celebrating an upcoming birth.

I will miss my husband regardless of whether or not a guest option is included on the invitation, whether or not I have a guest to consider, and whether or not I take a guest or go alone. It is nice to be included, and I need to practice keeping my awareness on the occasion and the people at hand.

30

Finding New Friends

WHEN MY THERAPIST suggested I find new friends, I balked. "Why do I need new friends? I have enough friends, and new friends will not fill my emptiness." But as I continued to feel hurt about not being invited or felt left out even when I *was* invited, I slowly came to realize how and why I needed to hear this instruction.

She was right. I did and do need new friends. While grieving I have lost some relationships and could certainly use some friends who are not part of a couple.

I still remain confused about the subgroup of friends who were there at first but then slowly moved away. Nothing dramatic happened between us. There were no angry words or misunderstandings—just a slow drifting until the time gap between gatherings became the most noticeable part of the relationship. I did not see it happening, only that it happened.

Did they intentionally leave? I do not think so anymore. I imagine they simply pulled back and then, as the months went by, the pullback created more space until a new habit was formed. With other people, I wonder if they found it hard to have a widow as a friend. Did they find it awkward to talk about their husbands? Was it difficult to be with me with their husbands at their sides? Was I too unhappy or moody? Were they preoccupied with their own problems? Or were they really more casual friends than I realized? I'm still not sure; I don't think I'll really ever know.

Although the reasons may differ in each case, the outcome is unfortunately the same: I have lost contact with several friends. I expected less frequent gatherings with many people we used to hang out with as a couple, but I notice fewer get-togethers with some of my individual friends who happen to be married too.

Of course, some of this loss is my doing. I pulled back from the couples and the group gatherings even when I was included. But not all of this change in my social network is coming from me.

At first I couldn't imagine making new friends at my age. In looking back I realize I haven't made many new friends in the last thirty years of my marriage. I was busy with work and children, the couples we knew, and my individual friends at work. I was rarely open to a new interaction with my limited time. I hardly had enough time to see the people already on my radar, never mind searching for new ones.

So, it is strange that, in fact, I *have* made a few new friends since becoming a widow. These include widows, divorcees, and married people. I did not plan to find new friends and did not acknowledge this need to myself until now.

So, how did it happen? In addition to the vacuum created by "friend flight," I experienced a slow change in my own attitude—openness for time and contact that I haven't had since having a family. Believe it or not, after spending too much time engrossed in overwhelming death-related details, I discovered more free time. Without my "we," I can now decide spontaneously to go out for dinner and more easily say yes to spur of the moment opportunities. I have only one calendar to review, and I can easily keep that one in my head.

I also find that new friends don't carry my memory baggage. With long-term friends, I may painfully remember "us." The unbidden images intrude when I least expect them. With a new person, these images are not there. I am faced with a different kind of regret, however, as these friends don't know my history and so only know part of me. I wish they had known him so they could share in my loss. Pictures and stories never do justice to the past.

So I end up with two distinct groups meeting different types of needs. The solid, ongoing friendships help me to hold my history and keep my identity intact. They help me to pre-serve the status quo with the least amount of disruption. In contrast, a few new friends give me hope for new interactions and eventually my changing identity.

What I can do for myself:

I need to let go of my friends who have distanced themselves while continuing to appreciate their role in the earlier phases of my life.

With my new friends, I can share more about my husband and family as I would when providing other parts of my personal history, such as where I grew up or how I lost my father. As I am increasingly able to discuss my husband with ease, others can more easily listen. My new friends will then have a more complete view of me.

I also can remain open to meeting other widows although I cannot guarantee friendship with someone simply because she is a widow.

31

Surgery Versus Loss

"Hey! I just called to see how the surgery went," says Rachel. "Can I stop by later? I made you lasagna!"

"I want to know when I can come by to hang out now that you are trapped in your house for a few weeks. Want me to bring a movie?" asks Mandy.

TEN MONTHS AFTER my husband's death, I had my hip replaced. I was in and out of the hospital very quickly and faced a few weeks of recovery at home. I was delighted with the support I received. People brought food, stopped by to watch me try to walk, and stayed to talk. It was almost enjoyable staying at home and having people drop by, as I didn't have to make efforts to have companionship. Even after I was walking normally again, people called to see how I was doing. During the following year people continued to ask me how my hip was progressing.

In comparison, they were less likely to ask me about how I was coping as a widow.

These reactions to my surgery thus presented a vivid contrast with those of the year before. I started thinking back to the weeks and months after he died. I remember often being alone. The frequency of social contacts seemed distinctly different for these two occasions.

This time the questions people asked me were almost exclusively centered on the surgery. There was a clear interest in my experience and my recovery. For a volume comparison, I believe I experienced a ten-to-one contrast: ten hip questions for every one question about managing widowhood. Or was it twenty-to-one? For quality of interactions, the post-hip scenario clearly was the winner.

When I was first widowed, many people kept their interactions with me quite brief. They would call, ask me how I was doing, and quickly get off the phone. I think they feared I might fall apart, and they would be locked into a long discussion. They wanted to prevent me from crying; they didn't want to open those floodgates.

After the loss of my husband, longer visits for an afternoon or evening seemed stressful for other people, and perhaps even for me. We often had the death elephant in the room that we dared not acknowledge. I remember times when people changed the topic, and I remember when they seemed to be chatting lightly, and sometimes aimlessly, to avoid direct talk of loss. They often had to go cook dinner or stop at the store rather than visit too long. They may have found it unnecessary to ask me how I was feeling. After all, they surely guessed how I felt. Both the frequency of the calls and the length of the visits seemed curtailed somehow to avoid letting the bad stuff out.

Of course, the prevailing moods during these two types of visits were certainly different. After a death, the tone and mood are, of course, particularly somber. After my husband died, other people had a serious tone that was perhaps difficult for them to endure. There was little room for humor or lightness, and the idea of focusing too long on grief was perhaps unpleasant to those visiting. To me it was simply my reality.

In contrast, after hip surgery, a serious tone was not required, and people were freer to be playful and joyous. Even the post-operative discomfort was clearly temporary and improving each day. Emotional reactions were not constrained by a grave event. A successful hip surgery can result in commiseration about pain, delight that the worst is over, and future plans for walking and hiking. Recovery can be celebrated, and relief is clearly defined.

In contrast, after a death, there is no clear marker of recovery, nothing to be cheerful about. The death of my husband leant itself only to unhappiness and worry about an uncertain future. Others might wonder, "What if it happens to me?" They weren't so worried about having a hip replaced.

This contrast between surgery and loss highlights part of the plight of those who sustain a personal tragedy. In our society we are ill-prepared and uneasy about how to speak to other people who have had a devastating death and equally ill-prepared to manage the traumas that happen to us personally. Those of us who directly sustain the loss end up interacting with well-meaning people but also with fumbling conversations, avoidance, and less support than we need.

What I can do for myself:

I can use more realistic self-talk to get myself through these contrasts and disappointments. People are not prepared to manage death, and their avoidance of me or the topic of loss does not signify a personal rejection. They may simply be rejecting the differing realities.

I can still enjoy the support for the surgery. I do not have to link or compare events, and I do not have to discount current support, regardless of whether it was there before or not.

32

I Had Already Said Yes

"I can't wait to see you! We will pick you up at noon."

I HAD ALREADY agreed to go to the art gallery with her on Saturday. When she called that morning to finalize the day, my jaw tightened as I heard her say, "we." At that moment I felt stuck. The "we" meant her husband was coming too. That "we" changed everything for me, but I said nothing.

I had already met my being-with-a-couple quota for the week. I didn't really have the energy for one more triangulated event. I had not planned and did not want to go to the gallery with a couple. But I told myself I could get through it, and I did.

I felt I had little choice as I had already said yes to the plan. I consulted with a friend about managing my dilemma, and she kindly suggested I could change my mind and simply not go. As I thought about bailing, I realized I just felt too awkward to suddenly announce I did not want to go. Of course, I could feign sickness, but that is really hard for me to do without a real illness. I could have said something else had come up, or I could have sighed that I had too much unanticipated work to complete. None of these last-minute excuses seemed plausible to pull off on such short notice. I find dishonest excuses take time to develop and require energy to deliver.

Telling the truth is easier with a pre-planned event. I have slowly learned to explain that I'm not up for a couples-based dinner or that I just don't have the energy to join a family for an outing. However, these explanations occur ahead of the activity, not plugged in suddenly at the last minute. As these expectations are set early, it seems to go fairly smoothly and nobody's feelings appear to get hurt. Or, at least so far this seems true.

It seems rude and quite childish to say the blunt truth, "I didn't know your husband was coming. I thought we were just spending time by ourselves. This change makes me not really want to go." I have thought these same thoughts at other times before becoming a widow. When I had made plans with a friend, I sometimes experienced disappointment to hear that now a partner or sister was coming. At the same time there have been occasions in which I did not mind it when other people were added on, and still other times when I relished the inclusion of others. For certain activities a group of people contributes to the liveliness and fun. However, since becoming a widow I more often experience extra folks as undesirable, especially if it is a partner now joining us.

What I can do for myself:

I am paying attention to my progress in this arena. I have adapted and shifted in my responsiveness. I am able to better tolerate being with couples than in the beginning, and I even enjoy myself sometimes. Still, these activities come with a certain amount of sadness. I want to continue to limit the amount and length of these threesome ventures. At the same time, I recognize I have come a long way from tolerating very few events with couples to probably a fifty-fifty rate of saying yes to invitations with couples.

I want to concentrate less on my single status and more on the relationships I do have and the activities I am doing. Yet, I do not want to push myself to say yes when I am self-consciously alone. It is fine if I continue to refuse some invitations, and it is fine if I am never comfortable in some group compositions. I do not need rigid rules of acceptable behavior; I need more fluid ones. And when plans change, even at the last minute, I reserve the right to change my mind.

33

The One-Year Mark

"Of course you are still miserable. It hasn't even been a year."

"You'll be okay after you go through this round of firsts."

"I know you'll feel better next year."

MANY WELL-MEANING PEOPLE readily share this truism with me. They have bought the American package, agreeing with a culture that tells us a year is enough, perhaps even too long, to mourn.

As a griever, I feel pressure to tow the line and follow the "normal" pattern. After this period of time, I believe others may begin to wonder if I'm too busy feeling sorry for myself or too needy to ever let go.

But my insides are churning and screaming that a year isn't nearly enough and I've just gotten started, perhaps not even *really* started. I am in preschool, not kindergarten, at this time. I am getting prepared for this hard knocks course, but I don't yet have the emotional stability or the prerequisite skills to make it.

Late at night when I think about how overwhelmed I can become with my grief, I remind myself that managing death is not viewed the same way by each person or every culture. While we encourage the grief-stricken to move on after a year, other cultures do not push this standard of time. In some societies, the opposite even occurs. People may be encouraged to stay in contact with those who have died, to continue the ongoing communication. Is one method really better than the next? Should we worry about the correct way to tackle our mourning?

Regardless of cultural differences, these "rules" for coping with death need to provide space for individual differences. Why should death and loss be any different than any other developmental transition? Not everyone begins to speak at the same age. Some read at age three while others not until age seven. Some graduate college in four years while others take eight years. Not everyone has 2.5 children, and many people now live with long-term partners without marriage. While we permit flexibility in other aspects of "normal" development, we seem to tamp down on grief.

Perhaps we have created stricter time norms for coping with death since loss and death are uncomfortable topics in our culture. We want to avoid facing these issues, and so we limit them however we can. Our culture helps us keep a lid on these tortuous themes. The one-year mandate helps by instructing us about when to move on. It's like a new head cold—only three days are acceptable or something more serious may be going on.

I find the notion of a one-year marker oppressive. I dread, rather than look forward to, the end of the first year without my husband. I find the proposed endpoint is stifling me and creating inner knots. This deadline has become a dark cloud over my internal calendar, adding strong guilt to my current range of emotions. As this anniversary approaches, I worry my legitimacy will dwindle.

I sometimes tell myself that it is a good sign that my despondency is still vividly present even as the year marker looms. I tell myself it's a sign of a strong relationship rather than the sign of an inadequate griever.

What are my options when my internal clock clashes with the framework of our society? I can buck the norm and continue focusing on my loss, or I can bow to social pressures. The first choice is not too popular. I find others are looking forward to the end of my year as they "know" I will then be on my way back to "normal."

I believe my friends are indeed relieved for the passage of time, and they hope I will not be so miserable as time rolls on. They don't know what to say if I spend too much energy on my loss, and they try to help me to see the good things happening in my current life. They definitely use this cutoff whether I do or not. Because these people are important to me, I don't always feel that I have as much choice as I'd like.

What I can do for myself:

I can acknowledge that timelines are indeed artificial and rarely a perfect fit for a given individual. Each one of us has our own issues to work out when we lose our life partner or experience any other significant loss. Different people have different experiences that therefore require unique amounts of processing time and various pathways.

I can accept some flexibility in my adjustment and in my view of myself as a widow.

34

I'm Sorry for Sharing My Grief . . . Again

"I'm okay now. Sorry, I was just having a bad time for a few minutes."

"Sorry to bring up my situation, had a brief dip, I guess."

"I'm sorry I sounded so down when we spoke earlier. I'm really fine, thanks."

I'M STILL OCCASIONALLY making this same mistake. These are the phrases I've said so often since my loss—the ways I take back my feelings, the ways I apologize for being too grouchy, or for sharing too much about my loss.

It is hard to keep all my thoughts and feelings inside my mind or even just inside the confines of my house. Even my dogs don't seem to listen anymore. After time has passed, most everyone is over it.

However, against my own better judgment and my resolve to be quiet, I still sometimes share my discouraged state of mind with other people. I may then call back to apologize, to say I'm okay. I hang up and tell myself to hold it in and keep quiet next time. Then the emotions build up, and I repeat the pattern.

What's going on here in this "here's how I feel/oh no, don't be burdened by me" dance. I'm overwhelmed by the bouts of grief that still hit me, a sticky wave that clings to my body as it refuses to flow away. I temporarily become engrossed in my unhappiness. As soon as I speak, my regret surfaces, and I am keenly aware of the adverse impact on my relationships. In spite of this awareness, however, I find myself repeating this pattern.

I'm not even sure that talking about my loss helps anymore, and yet I sometimes have the urge to continue. I know I am obsessively stating the same pathetic speech—the review of my empty house and lack of close contact, how much I miss him, how my life is derailed and my future less certain. I even get bored with my own descriptions at times.

I really am sorry to those I may drag down when my distress jumps out of my mouth. Sometimes they just listen which helps me get it out of my system, and I get a few minutes of pause and relief, but at what cost? I'm sure they are tired of my recurring negativity.

When others make suggestions to help me get out of my state of funk, I resist their ideas to try a new activity, see a doctor, get outside, or read a good book. While these ideas may be useful, my replies are often "I can't" or "I won't" or simply "not yet" . . . and then "I'm sorry."

As I reflect on this cycle of behavior—negative comments followed by apology—I see a pattern that is common for many situations for many of us. Think of how we make plans to exercise; resolutions to eat healthier; desires to cut down smoking or drinking; promises to try harder, to not do it again, whatever the "it" is. We all promise, we plan, we hope, and we swear to do it differently next time. Yet we fall victim again and again of stress, fatigue, the superpowers of emotions, or simply force of habit. The apologies, to both others and to ourselves, are sincere but often short-lived. The urge of strong emotions increases while the willpower and resolve decrease.

My unexpected outpouring of grief followed by "I'm sorry" is one more example of a somewhat unsuccessful effort to alter a personal pattern.

What I can do for myself:

I can recognize how difficult it is to change most behaviors and therefore acknowledge that this struggle to break free of this pattern applies to me as well as to others.

At the same time, I can notice the progress I am making by the spaces between my discouraging comments. I really do have more time between the flood and the mopping up. If this undesirable pattern continues, I may return to my own personal therapy.

35

My Decision Tree: Go for Them or Choose for Me

IT IS 7:40 at night, and I was invited to a party that starts in twenty minutes. I put my coat on to head out and find I can't get myself to step outside the door, not even to drop by for a few minutes. I close the door and sit back down.

I can picture the other people enjoying the laughter and the beer, and I cannot maintain a picture of myself in this place. I briefly try to imagine it would be just fine to go, but this thought is quickly hijacked by my ongoing social awkwardness. After a few minutes I take my coat off and turn on the computer.

Is this selfishness on my part? Should I be going even if I don't want to? I've asked myself these questions often in response to many opportunities, and I've analyzed many of my refusals since becoming a widow. When I attend, I often feel awkward, wishing I had stayed home. When I opt out and stay home, I frequently feel guilty. Of course there are times when I push myself and I'm okay with being there and other times when I am glad I stayed home. However, there have not yet been enough of the glad-I-went experiences to convince me to go tonight.

I tell myself that feeling selfish, or rather self-focused, may still be just fine. I need ongoing space to continue to process my not-so-new circumstances. Operating as a single person still exhausts me and social interactions continue to take up more energy than I'd like.

To manage these dilemmas, I have created a new decision tree to use when I can't decide to say yes or no to a social invitation. It is broader than my previous focus simply on the number of couples, or whether or not other single people will be present. I have named the process "I go for them, or choose for me."

I start by asking myself, "What is the purpose of this event?" After this basic question there are two main branches. For the right branch, the occasion is to honor someone else. In these instances I will push myself to attend. I went to the retirement party and the 90th birthday celebration, and I plan to be at that wedding. Those events are focused on other people. Even if I really don't want to go, I will still go. I no longer think twice about these decisions. Saying yes is the right thing to do.

If the event is an occasion without an honoree, I move to the left side of the decision tree. This side has additional branches depending on the size of the gathering. One sub-branch addresses very large social gatherings. In these instances, the decision to attend depends solely on my choice. Here's where I give myself complete permission to say no. If going is awkward and not going won't bother anyone else, I can say no without guilt. I often use this branch for parties that include many couples.

With smaller groups, the decision about going becomes more complicated, even without an honored guest. If only five or six people are invited, I may feel compelled to show up, even if I'm the only single person going. My absence would be noticed, and I do not want to disappoint others. My decision here, therefore, varies with the occasion, the specific people, and my state of mind.

What I can do for myself:

I can continue to use this decision tree. This guide has reduced my discomfort when I receive social invitations. Having this scheme lends a reasonable rationale to my decisions and makes me feel better about them.

Of course I realize my tree is likely to change over time. I remain open to revising my decision patterns and adding new criteria and even new branches.

36

Attending a Funeral

I MUST GO whether I want to or not. A friend's father has died, and I need to be there for her family. This is not about me. However, going to my first funeral since my husband died is particularly hard as I pile my own memories onto her new loss.

Before the actual day, I imagined what it would be like. I would see anguish and tears, hear comforting words, and observe reunions of long lost relatives and friends. I would see the flowers, sign the guest book, and join the rows of people waiting for the immediate family to enter. I cried in advance for my own memories of my husband's memorial service and then I practiced how to steel myself. I talked to myself, reminding myself that I could not let the tears of my own loss overshadow their loss. I needed to manage these very intense triggers.

I had failed at a similar task when I was younger. In the 1980s, I went to a friend's funeral a few years after my father had died. She was not a close friend, but I was unable to contain my tears and emotions. I found my mind jumped right back to my father's funeral, and I was stunned with anguish and disbelief. I spent time at this funeral fighting with myself to try to maintain a bit of decorum. I was exhausted afterwards.

I did better this time, although, as before, I was tired when I returned home from the energy of managing my internal turmoil. Of course I am older and now have attended more funerals. I knew what to do by offering hugs, being silent and listening. I knew what to say by simply acknowledging the loss. And more importantly, I knew what not to say, such as, "It will get better after time passes" or "At least his suffering has ended."

During this funeral, one helpful thing surprised me. People who I had not seen for a while made empathetic comments to me. It was strange to feel increased support at a time that I dreaded. Two or three people came up to me and said how they realized how difficult my loss must have been. The intensity of the moment somehow brought out their thoughts and their words. I didn't know what to say. However, I really valued their support.

Going to this funeral helped me to recognize the community spirit that goes into grieving. We become more sensitive to issues of loss whenever a new loss presents itself, and more camaraderie may result. Even at funerals for other people, we may find comfort for our personal situation.

What I can do for myself:

So I did better this time due to my planning and practice. I was better able to respond to their loss without jumping into my own vortex of grief. My pre-tears and practice worked to get me through the funeral and the equally grueling reception. I have learned from being on the other side and know better how to respond. I can use these strategies for future situations in which tremendous grief is present.

Of course, part of my success reflects the fact that more time has passed since my loss and I'm less torn up inside on a regular basis. I modulate my emotions more easily and am able to set them aside. Nonetheless I still had to allow myself time to re-grieve and then to recover again after the funeral, knowing the struggle inside zaps my reserves.

37

Many Questions Without Many Answers

"What are your plans?"

"Are you selling your house?"

"Are you going to keep working?"

"Will you move to be near your children?"

"What's keeping you here?"

THESE QUESTIONS LEAVE me questioning and doubting: "I should move because I don't need this house; I have no reason to stay here, but I don't know where I want to go; I need a new life plan; I should decide about work and my finances; I should know what is next..." However, I don't know any of these things. I have no clear answers.

These questions and my lack of answers create stress for me. Do other people figure these things out? How do they do it? When do they do it? Why can't I do it?

I reassure myself by remembering that timing and planning are such personal things. Just because Sarah started dating after a year or Laura bought a more "manageable" condo does not mean these decisions are right for me. I know there are millions of paths as I travel though grief, and my path is, obviously, not yet decided. There is no timetable for correctness and certainly no resolution around the corner.

Yet, still, when others ask these questions, I experience self-doubt. These well-meaning queries add to my discomfort and my confusion. I wonder if I'm behind in my plans and not keeping pace with my personal tragedy. I am sure my turmoil is immediately apparent on my face and others probably wished they hadn't asked.

I do see the value, however, in raising the questions. Perhaps even my panic at hearing these questions shows me their relevance. Left alone, without being asked, I might not push myself to think about where I am headed or what I want for myself. Perhaps it is time to start thinking about the questions themselves, even without any immediate answers.

Truthfully, I've been living mostly in limbo since my husband died, and I am still not completely ready to commit to anything new. I maintain my sense of self by continuing to rely on my memories of my relationship and my family, incorrectly seeing my current state as a temporary phenomenon. My identity often remains fixed in who I was, how I was, and the former details of everyday life. The required transition feels like an outside pressure from which I vigorously shield myself. Avoidance and denial remain my friends right now, and I am not ready to completely kick them out.

It is hard to give up something without having something to replace it with. Giving up my living-in-the-past mentality is difficult when I really liked the old way of being and don't have a better vision to fill in the gaps. I imagine an unbearable hole if I start to move forward. I know everyone told me to wait a while before changing my plans or direction, but now that a year has passed I feel pressure to have some answers. I want to begin considering possible scenarios. The past is never going away, but I still want to begin charting the time ahead.

What I can do for myself:

When asked these difficult questions I can pause, observe my immediate defensiveness, and then simply respond, "Those are important questions I am just starting to tackle." In this way I acknowledge that these questions are helpful and reasonable, but don't pressure myself for an immediate answer. I give myself the space and time I need to consider future options.

PART THREE

Over Time

THIS THIRD GROUP of essays was written "Over Time," sometime after a year and into the second, third, and even the fourth year after becoming a widow, when most other people figured I had, or should have, moved on.

In this phase I have made progress but still remain stuck too much of the time. At the beginning of this phase, my grief was more palpable, but, as the months passed, the intense pain began to recede more often. I have moved from my original stuck-grief to a more subtle type of ongoing grief, a work in progress without a conclusion.

The frequency of my profound dips has lessened, but the dips themselves can still throw me off balance. I have become more reliable in my moods but can readily hit bottom given the right combination of triggers, such as thinking of a shared vacation spot, reviewing family photographs, or considering growing older alone.

Conversations with other folks have returned primarily to pre-loss content and flavor. People rarely ask me about being a widow and don't mention my late husband too often. When he is mentioned, I find it easier to speak about him and share memories of our life together.

During this third phase, I have been spending a little more time with other folks who are single and even tried dating. Most of the time I accept that my life must move forward, in spite of missing my husband and my former married life. At the same time, I have learned to enjoy more of my time alone.

I think of my grief as a lifelong process of adjustment. I know it may never go away, but as time and new experiences have been added, my grief has begun to lose its central role and step aside. I am slowly overcoming the social awkwardness of being a widow.

38

They Don't Even Know I'm a Widow

I WAS WITH a friend at a coffee shop when I met someone new. My friend introduced me to her friend in the usual way, and then we exchanged names and a few basics, such as where we live and work, and how we both know our friend in common. After returning home, I found myself feeling slightly melancholy. At first I wasn't sure why. Then it hit me—the new person doesn't even know I'm a widow.

It is interesting that this non-information has become so important to me. Before my loss, I never announced being married to other people. I was confident within myself and often did not mention my marital status. When the topic of my marriage became a topic within a conversation, it was simply a natural progression of sharing. It did not have to come first or even come at all sometimes. It was not necessarily in the forefront of getting to know a new person.

The time I spend deciding whether or not to share my status as a widow tells me that this new status still defines me. Soon after my loss, I did not want anyone to know I was a widow. At first I was in too much turmoil to discuss it, and after several months, I was embarrassed to be a widow. I was self-conscious about my loss and aware of how uncomfortable people became when I discussed the death of my husband. Later on there were times when I unintentionally blurted out my widow status but regretted it later. Now I've changed once again. I often *do* want them to know. What is this change in me about?

There are several reasons that I want to tell other people that I lost my husband. Unfortunately, one of the reasons is that part of me still wants other people to feel sorry for me. I want to share my unrelenting hurt so others will appreciate my loss. I want their sympathy to validate my ongoing unhappiness. I also find remembering my marriage helps me to manage my uncomfortable and still unfamiliar single status.

At the same time, however, my decision to intentionally share my widow identity reflects my improved adjustment. I can now discuss my loss as a fact without appearing overwhelmed. It has become safer for me to bring up the topic. During the first few months, I teared up instantly whenever I discussed my husband, and my intense reaction made others squirm. Now that I can describe this loss with a neutral tone of voice, others accept this fact in stride. I am actually freer to discuss my loss than I was in the first year after he died.

What I can do for myself:

I can continue to notice my fluctuating state of mind with regard to acknowledging that I'm a widow. I then can decide, in a particular situation, if it is helpful or not to share my widow identity, as it is my choice and my responsibility. When I decide to share, I can quickly move on without sidetracking a conversation.

If I am simply seeking sympathy, I realize it is time to let that go. People must confront many difficult situations and losses. While my loss remains profound to me, I know others are confronting other sources of pain as well.

If sharing my widowhood is more descriptive than emotional, then it is acceptable to share my widowed status as part of my personal introduction. However, it does not need to be disclosed right away when I meet someone new. I can wait for them to know this aspect of my life.

39

Post-Vacation Blues

"Did you have a great time on your vacation?" asks Marianna. "So glad you got away for a good break."

I JUST RETURNED from a vacation, and it is true I'm glad I went. I loved being with my former college friends and seeing new places out west. It was a break, and it was nice to get away.

In predictable fashion, I came back and shared details of my adventures and showed photos from my outings to Marianna and others. I had a good vacation and a nice opportunity to share happiness when I returned. I eagerly asked about her vacation too and enjoyed hearing about, and seeing, other parts of the west coast from her trip.

However, amidst these shared joys I also experienced a secondary letdown reaction inside.

Of course, nobody asked me how it felt to return home after a vacation. I suppose this is not a question that anyone asks, as we all assume it is hard to get back to the daily grind after a trip. Although I keep hoping it will go away, a part of me experienced an increase in distress after this adventure. This trip was my first two-weeker since my husband died, and the strain of returning was greater than after weekend retreats. When I came home from this lengthy vacation, reality greeted me again and it, of course, included the fullness of my loss. While I was away in a new environment, it was easier to put my misery aside. I was out of my daily world and happier than I have been in a long time, but I felt myself sinking back to a more unhappy state of mind as I returned.

Of course the vacation was not a total relief. I still experienced blue times when I remembered past vacations. But overall this time away provided a needed change of scenery that helped me live in the present.

Even the post-vacation sharing of photographs and details provided an escape and a glimpse of moving on. I had new experiences in my new state of being, and they have started to make an inroad on my sense of self. On vacation, part of my widow identity was gone for a while, and I have to admit that was a welcome relief.

What I can do for myself:

I can still share the joys of my vacation but also can accept that the post-vacation blues are normal, with or without a significant loss. It is unreasonable to expect people to ask me about my return feelings, but I can acknowledge to myself the difficult readjustment. I can remind myself that there are more times of happiness in the years to come.

40

Managing Plural Pronouns

"Next week we're going to . . ."

"Wait until you hear what happened to us . . ."

"We will . . ." "We won't . . ." "We . . ."

I'M IN THE middle of a casual conversation when I hear these simple words. The plural pronouns jump out to grab me, even when I don't focus on them. It's the emphasis on words that signify couples, spouses, and partners, and the actual words that follow the "we" are irrelevant. When I first became a widow I discovered the power of this "couple-talk" and soon developed an aversion to references to "we" and "us." These pronouns continued to highlight the chronic emptiness of my ongoing widowed status.

After a few months I noticed these words more often than immediately after my loss. When I first lost my husband, people avoided obvious references to their spouse or partner. I don't remember hearing the awful "we" and "us" words as frequently. Now, however, for most people, our exchanges have returned to normal. Occasionally they may consider my widowed state, but it is no longer in the foreground. People freely discuss their families and their relationships, as if my disruption did not happen.

Of course, I don't want people to alter normal conversations or limit the content or depth of their conversations around me. I value intimacy, and telling others I remain bothered by their use of "we" and "us" will surely stifle the conversations. However, I do want others to not forget about my loss and to be just a little bit more careful. I wish they would reduce the frequency of references to their partners and coupled activities in my presence.

It is natural to make social comparisons. We do it all the time. I walk into a friend's house and notice how much cleaner it is than mine. I listen to a work discussion and notice how much more my colleague knows about a topic. Conversely, I may feel guilty for having more vacation time than a family member and may downplay my knowledge on a topic. Our relative haves and have-nots provide an ongoing context for what we share and how we share it. Since my husband died, I started making pronoun comparisons. They would share "we" and "us" while I could only say "I."

Although I remain sensitive to partner-focused references, in this recent phase of my grief I have made progress in my own use of these same plural pronouns. Right after my loss I would correct myself; I would start to say "we" and then would say, "I mean I." Now I am more likely to use my own couple-talk by referring to my personal history—including my marital history—in current conversations. My "we" is in the past but still important to share. I am becoming more comfortable providing memories of our life together.

The process of life review is often used by adults to reflect on their accomplishments from the past and maintain a cohesive lifespan identity. In a similar way, as a widow, I can recall shared life events as part of the fabric of my own relationship review. This past tense sharing of my relationship signals my improved self-acceptance.

What I can do for myself:

When the plural pronouns still bother me, I might gently redirect a conversation, but this approach can only be used occasionally. Instead I want to keep increasing my own use of these pronouns by sharing more of my personal history. I can choose to join couple-focused topics by recounting activities I did with my late husband.

41

Reducing and Redirecting My Social Needs

Carina asks, "Want to join a group of women for movie night on Wednesday?"

I respond, "I think I'll pass, but thanks for thinking of me."

I DO THIS —refuse, that is—more and more often. The old pre-widowed me might have quickly said yes to an event such as this. Now, I decline more social invitations, even those without an emphasis on couples. I ask myself if this changing pattern represents ongoing sadness or a new vision of myself. I'd like to think it is the latter.

As a consequence of losing my daily partner, I have been forced to spend more time alone. I'm almost always by myself in the late evening and when not at work. Of course I meet friends for lunch, attend workshops, go out of town to visit relatives, chat on the phone a lot, and participate in some social gatherings. However, if I added up and compared my alone time versus time with others, I assume my time alone has tripled or quadrupled compared to my pre-loss lifestyle. Even if my children lived in town or if I had many single friends, I think this contrast would be evident.

At first I really disliked any time alone. It highlighted my loss and my loneliness. I wasn't sure what to do with myself with this sudden increase in unplanned time. I was miserable having nobody to discuss the day with. My alone time was often grief time. I sometimes sat and did nothing or played online games as I watched the time pass.

Slowly, however, I have learned to fill the increased hours. In fact, lately I notice I'm actually lacking time. It's hard to believe, but I actually could use more time. In addition to writing this book, I read the news more online, work out more regularly, clean up more often, and have a list of unfinished projects from photo books to updating my website. I actually am disappointed in the evening when I realize it is after 10 p.m. and I have accomplished little on my list.

Part of this appreciation of my time alone probably represents my adjustment to being on my own. As my depressed feelings from widowhood have become less pervasive, I am more productive. However, I don't think reduced grief is the only factor in my attitude change.

I remember learning that people at midlife may experience a shift and develop untapped sides of themselves. A change in our perspective of time may reflect a developmental transition. While changing our point of view from youth-based with an unending future to a midlife view with a limited future, we may alter our priorities. As part of this balancing of energy, some introverts become more interested in engaging with other people and some extroverts reawaken their desire for self-reflection or solo activity. For many of us advancing past midlife, time becomes more precious. I may have naturally turned away from my extroverted bent to a more balanced lifestyle.

So I don't know if my increased focus on making the most of my time alone is natural aging or a sign of adjustment. I assume it must be some combination. I hope I will maintain some of my increased appreciation of time spent alone, even if my social contacts expand in the future.

What I can do for myself:

I can acknowledge that some of the adjustments from becoming a widow could have a favorable outcome. As changes in myself occur over time, I want to maintain this broader frame of reference.

42

It's Getting Easier to Host

RIGHT AFTER HE died I thought I'd never host again. As time passed, however, the quiet of the empty house challenged me. After a year of limiting my social life to "elsewhere," I felt a desire to have people right here, in my home. I needed more laughter and voices close around me.

At first, I limited myself to one person at a time. A friend might come in before picking me up, or I'd invite someone over for coffee. This one-person-limit sometimes bothered me by reminding me of what I was missing, but it also helped me to fill some of the void.

After a while, however, I took another step: I invited a couple over for dinner. Of course, I started with people I know well in case it was awkward or I could not pull it off. I found planning alone was tiring and stressful. In addition to intentionally creating a threesome for dinner, I felt relieved when they left. It was strange to be the odd one out in my own house. This strain of initiating and hosting saddened me, but I was relieved that I had made an effort.

In spite of this discouragement, I rallied my energy several months later and invited another couple to dinner. I found it was a little easier this time, but again, after they left, the loneliness haunted me. I could hear them laughing and talking on the way to their car, and inside I sank.

Yet, I didn't give up. I made sure I had fresh coffee, bought the cream everyone else likes, and tried to keep the kitchen cleaner. I became more and more comfortable inviting friends to come in.

My new efforts to socialize continue to remind me of the gatherings my husband and I had hosted together. One of our main events was an annual New Year's Eve party. I remember spending lots of time cleaning and planning. After a few hours of socializing, the group crammed into the living room for a "steal the gift" exchange followed by a champagne toast when the ball dropped at midnight in Times Square.

The last time we hosted this party it was 8:15, and nobody had arrived yet for the 8 p.m. start time. All the food was on the table, and my husband and I were watching TV, waiting for our first guests to arrive. I distinctly remember turning to him and saying, "What if nobody shows?" Although I really didn't think this would happen, my anxiety over hosting invariably emerged. I will never forget his confident reply: "If nobody comes, we'll enjoy a lot of good food!" I smiled, breathed a sigh of relief, and sat back to relax. In this way, he was the root of my social confidence, helping me to know we could host a party without worrying about the outcome.

Although I'm not yet ready to organize another New Year's Eve party, I am taking my hosting to new heights. This year I invited a group of close friends to a dessert party one evening over the holidays. It was a fourteen-person gathering, significantly smaller than the former gala event, but definitely a major step toward reclaiming and opening my house to larger groups.

Who knows what I may host next year?

What I can do for myself:

I'm doing all I can at this point. I have ventured past my comfort zone to invite others into my home the way I used to. It isn't as easy or as comfortable as it was when I was half of a couple, but I'm proceeding nonetheless. I am pushing myself to recapture aspects of my former lifestyle, although it will never be exactly the same.

I can expand my step-by-step approach, knowing I will soon be okay with hosting more often. I still am not ready for a large gathering, but perhaps one day my comfort and confidence will return and larger events will once again be part of my repertoire.

43

Entering the Dating Pool

"I have a divorced friend in town for a few days. Want to meet him?"

"Let me think about it . . ."

Several days later, I say, "Okay, I think I'd like to meet him, but let's keep it really casual."

FILLED WITH HESITATION, anxiety, and misgivings, I have put my toes into the dating pool. Although I lack confidence and conviction, I've decided it's time to test the waters, time to see who's out there. I don't know if there's a new relationship in my future or not, and I remain unsure if this is what I want.

My friends seem both surprised and relieved. I've been stuck in grief for so long that sadness has become my normal countenance, my go-to way of being. Since going on some casual dates, I can share the highs and lows of these occasions, and this adds a new lightness to my end of conversations. My discussion of dating has helped my social interactions to be more present, even more future oriented.

However, this step into the future is fraught with many complex feelings. In some ways, meeting other men makes me miss my husband even more. I miss the ease and relaxation of being with someone predictable, a situation where love and commitment are taken for granted. Being with someone new, even for a brief coffee meet-and-greet, requires manufactured conversations, lots of questions, and energy I often don't have.

Of course this is not how my relationship with my husband started. My own search pattern has changed drastically. In my early adult years, the pattern was as follows: I would be attracted to men, have conversations with them, and then pursue getting to know them. I didn't worry initially about whether we had a future together. I was young, and there was no rush. Many of the issues my husband and I faced in our marriage did not even appear until we had been a couple for several years. Perhaps our naïveté—not knowing all the potential problems ahead of time— contributed to a we-can-work-it-out attitude. In contrast, as a seasoned adult, I am pre-checking criteria before saying hello. I consider political ideology and whether they like dogs before meeting them in person. Information, not feelings, now determines the people I meet.

Online dating procedures are directing my new dating approach. I check first and act second. Like my online comrades, I have posted my interests and a few important values. I posted a photo that was recent and acceptable. I don't know how significant these details really are, but I find it reassuring that the procedures are established for me to follow. I have discussed basic information over a secure email site and have actually met a few men this way.

As I read descriptions of available men and scan photos for signs of warmth and intelligence, I worry about my age and dating. I don't want to waste my precious time with people I don't care for. However, to find special folks, I know there may be a difficult, probably time-consuming selection process.

In addition to missing the familiarity of a life partner, new anxieties spring to the surface when I contemplate searching for men to date. I haven't worried for a long time if either I like the other person or if the other person likes me. With friends, there is an initial getting-connected phase, but the potential for rejection is muted compared to dating. I must now be ready to hear, "We're not a match" or be ready to deliver those same words. I was recently informed via an online exchange that I had an "incompatible astrological sign," and I felt amused rather than rejected. It is hard to feel rejected by an individual I've never met.

Embarrassment also is prominent in my consideration of how and where to meet a date. One of the first men I met lived out of town, and that made the awkwardness a little easier. In my second effort, I met a man in a small sandwich shop in the middle of the week. As I entered the restaurant, I found myself looking around, worried about seeing someone I know. I was ashamed to be seen with a new person. I felt like a traitor to my husband. I felt a need to prepare an explanation of why I was having coffee with a stranger. This urge to justify to those who knew my husband keeps me searching for out-of-the-way meeting spots. My desire to hide new encounters suggests I'm not completely ready to go on dates, or perhaps I need practice to get ready.

I worry about my lack of skills and flexibility. In a long-term marriage, I became accustomed to certain ways of doing things—how to enjoy the evening, planning vacations, and even discussing money. I now imagine adapting to new life-styles and daily activities. I feel somewhat wary anticipating such adjustments. I remind myself it could be fun, or at least interesting, instead of work.

I worry what to do if dating goes beyond the initial meeting. How do I know if I like someone? Can I ever care about another man the way I cared about my husband? Will it simply be different? I want to be able to discuss my husband, to be able to savor my marriage and a new relationship at the same time. I want the past loves of our lives to be part of a new interaction. I'd like to form a new relationship without replacing my former one.

What I can do for myself:

I can accept that dating is awkward. I may need to seek support from other women who are divorced or have lost their partners and have ventured out again. I want to hear their thoughts, disappointments, and successes.

I also can approach this phase with curiosity and the possibility of enjoyment. However, I need to be happy by myself, even as I seek to find new relationships.

44

Unfortunate Grief Replacement

My friend Candice hasn't seen me in a while. I bump into her in a store, and she naturally asks, "How are you doing?"

I answer, "I'm overwhelmed with family illnesses right now. Let me tell you what's going on . . ."

ILLNESSES AND DIRE situations recently struck my family. My mother has declined and is in need of more services, supervision, and interventions. Around the same time, two relatives died, and my aunt was diagnosed with life threatening kidney cancer. As a result, conversations with my relatives increased in frequency and intensity. My world has once again been thrust into an emphasis on survival, pressured decision making, and a sense of alarm.

As a result of these present health emergencies and recent losses, my personal widow-based grief is relegated to the back seat out of sheer necessity. There is only so much turmoil my brain and body can tolerate. I have watched my loss recede into the background, joining the ranks of the troubles from my past. The current anguish overrides the chronic pain of my grief, as it should.

As I reflect on this grief replacement process, part of me resists. Sometimes I hold tight to the grief of being a widow to keep my memories with my husband vibrant and current. However, in addition to the passage of time, I now have new, urgent forces diminishing my loss.

In response to these changing circumstances, the topics in my conversations with family and friends have shifted. When I spend time with family members, we now discuss the current health crises. We no longer converse about my loss or their issues as the present preoccupations take over. Similarly with my close friends, I share more about these newer problems and less about my ongoing loneliness. I bring up what is foremost on my mind.

I believe our present lives are more important than the details of the past. While we may mourn losses or aversive family events from early on, what stands out as most important are those events that directly impact daily life. My present concerns have rightfully become the most important aspects of my life, what I must tackle today. My loneliness is temporarily assigned to a dimly illuminated place outside the current spotlight.

These new crises have altered the intensity of my grief. When the current crises subside, I imagine my grief will again say, "Here I am." I need to be comfortable with this in-and-out pattern of changing attention.

What I can do for myself:

I would like to accept that this is how it all works. As time moves on, new issues arise that take precedence over prior loss. I can manage my present life, even while my underlying grief persists. I do not need to feel guilty about refocusing. It is the right thing to do.

45

My Improved Pattern of Grief

MOST OF THE time nobody knows. I'm going along like I'm healed, appearing as if nothing is amiss. New people I meet don't know my history of loss and most often have no clue about my ongoing unrest.

On rare occasions, however, while I'm engaged in an activity or in the midst of a conversation, I find myself suddenly fighting back tears. Most of the time now I am able to recover quickly, and the fleeting tears dry. My personal struggle stays personal.

However, on rare occasions—just as I did "In the Beginning"—I become too overwhelmed to censor my reactions, and the dam breaks. I want to explain the current pattern of my grief, even after a few years have passed.

My new pattern of grief is less frequent but hard hitting when it happens. The pain of my loss has sometimes moved over but is still within striking distance. I no longer have the reality of his death pressed against my face on a 24/7 basis. I don't feel sick all the time. However, during those episodes when my misery races to the surface, it comes with a fierce, sometimes uncontrollable, intensity. It shakes me as before, although I do enjoy lengthier quiet periods during the interim.

I had not anticipated this pattern or this outcome. Before all this happened, I thought grief would gradually dissipate. I thought my sadness would follow a slow but steady decline. I didn't expect these attacks of misery, or the quiet interludes.

When change is gradual, we can more easily adjust along the way. When we slowly increase our debt, collect household items one at a time, or gradually get older, our adaptations seem automatic and barely noticeable. We may look back and wonder how we got from there to here, but along the way the process seems less noticeable than if we quickly amass a large debt, suddenly have a closet stuffed with junk, or had failed to notice our yearly birthdays.

Grief doesn't always follow this rule of adaptation. Prompted by random interactions and memories—a person I haven't seen in a while, a royal blue-colored t-shirt, or advertisements for camping equipment—grief may leap out against my will and freely grab me on its own timetable.

These less frequent but intense displays throw me off-base. I may be able to squelch the urge to cry and continue to smile, but my energy is depleted in the process. I may appear preoccupied or less involved in the conversation. In a few minutes I return but find I may repeat a question that was just answered or ask again for a story already told. I sometimes lose my place.

What I can do for myself:

Whatever the pathway of grief, I can assume it is normal for me. It may change again over time, but for now, I can explain the evolution of my misery from constant to variable. I can warn close family and friends that I have not finished the mourning process and that my less often but still hard-hitting pattern represents improvement.

I must be patient with myself as I recognize the stock market picture of grief with its erratic course, high points, and dips. I still invest in the financial stock market in spite of its tumultuous trajectory. Similarly, I invest in my up-and-down pattern of recovery and a more positive future.

Conclusion

I HAVE MADE progress in managing my grief, but I'm still in it—grief, that is—for the long haul. I don't see the full sadness being erased any time soon. I don't cry as easily as I used to, and I'm not thinking about him or my widowhood all the time. Yet the specter of our life together and the specific, daily life interactions that I miss so much still haunt me more often than I'd like to admit.

I have seen firsthand the enormous social pain of being suddenly single, and I have spent too much time recoiling from day-to-day interpersonal interactions. I am still bothered by the situations in this book, but the intensity of being bothered has decreased. I've gained insight into my own weaknesses and vulnerabilities. I have used some of my own ideas and ignored others. I assume I am recovering the best I can.

I don't remember the first six months or perhaps the whole first year much at all. When I wasn't in acute despair, I was numb. I somehow went through the motions, but the details remain a blur. I think I was half-conscious or simply functioning on autopilot. Writing these essays helped to ground me, forcing me to reflect on where I was stuck and where I was changing.

As time has passed, I have forgotten many personal details about my husband and our life together. I can't always clearly remember what happened or what he said on a given occasion. My resources are the voicemails, pictures, some videos, and the memories shared with my children, but vagueness occasionally takes over my memories. Sometimes I hold on to my loss for fear of losing more memories and a larger piece of my identity as his wife and partner.

I have asked myself what would happen if and when I could really move on. In many ways this option does not seem fair or right. Why do I get to move on and he doesn't? Survivor guilt hits me.

This whole ordeal of losing my husband and becoming a widow has changed me as well as my social interactions. I think differently about life, about myself, about money, and about the people with whom I want to interact. I value time in a new way and intentionally avoid doing things I don't really want to do or spending too much time with those I consider only casual friends. Is this just a natural consequence of my rude awakening or simply my adjustment to becoming older and being more careful with my time? I'm not sure.

Others may notice these changes and not like them. I may lose some more friends, not just because of being a widow, but because I've lost some of my ability to be carefree and optimistic.

Not everyone wants to think about our limited lifetimes, and being with a widow may highlight that reality, especially being with a widow who is less light-hearted.

At the same time some good things have happened as well. I have deepened long-term friendships and made a few new friends. As I change and hopefully grow, I am having more conversations that are complex and more meaningful. Sometimes my focus on the larger picture helps me to be more accepting of the differences among friends and relatives as I challenge myself to move forward. I need others to be real, but that does not mean they must be similar to me.

I have also become a better friend to myself. I have increasingly mastered doing things for and by myself. In spending more time alone, I have had perhaps too much time to reflect, but eventually some of this reflection has paid off. I am becoming clearer regarding what is important and why, as I've learned to appreciate who I am. As I learn what I want and need, to both give and to get, I am also trying to have better interpersonal relationships, to be a better friend.

I believe I've learned to respond more effectively to loss. I know better what to say and what not to say to others experiencing profound grief. I know my particular process of mourning has been impacted by my age, where I live, the marital status of my support network, and by my personal expectations and social needs. While I realize that other widows may not share all my feelings or experiences, I'm sure we have loneliness and panic in common. I now act more quickly when others face a loss. I call sooner, attend the funeral, and whenever possible, try to offer immediate help, a ride or a meal, rather than "words of wisdom."

In conclusion, I hope the thoughts, feelings, and experiences shared in these essays are helpful to you and other widows. I know we each have unique situations and different strategies to manage our new social interactions as we adapt to this new phase of life. I hope each of us finds a meaningful path forward.

A Note to Supporters

I WAS IN a getting-to-know-you conversation with another widow and two married men. We were introducing ourselves and sharing what we were doing, including work and creative activities. One person was starting a new business, and one had recently retired and was taking art classes. As part of my own introduction, I shared this writing project and then heard the usual request for examples of social discomfort.

I briefly listed a few of the interpersonal situations that left me feeling awkward. I described being invited to all-couples dinners, not being called on weekend nights, and the aggravation I felt when others compared their losses to mine. As I described these situations, one of the men began to counter each of my examples. "Well, I'm sure your friends didn't mean that." And "After all, it is a world of couples. What's wrong with going alone?" While he was talking, I noticed the other widow was looking directly at me and affirmatively nodding her head. After he had finished speaking, she clearly stated, "I know exactly what you mean, Eileen. I have even more examples of stressful social interactions."

This pattern was repeated many times. Many people defended the other people in my scenarios. If I said I wished people would call on weekends, they remarked that other people had families they needed to be with on weekends. If I said people were encouraging me to count my blessings, they commented, "Others are just trying to make you feel better." If I said I was asked to bring a guest to a wedding, they quickly pointed out that the hosts were being inclusive. Thus, I heard counter arguments when others listened to the topics I was experiencing and writing about. In response to their opposing comments, I typically spent several minutes explaining that I was not intending to criticize anyone, that I had said many of these same statements in the past, but nonetheless such points of view were not often helpful.

The purpose of this book is to highlight interpersonal situations and dilemmas from the perspective of the new widow, rather than the point of view of the other people in her life. So, if you are reading this book as a support person and not a survivor, please realize that all of us try to make grievers feel better. Sometimes we think the best thing is to change the subject, sometimes we think it is most helpful to point out the positive events, and sometimes we think we connect best by sharing a loss we have experienced. Other times our own needs come first, and we can't really say anything helpful, and on still other occasions we are able to just listen. Interactions are just that—imperfect interactions. The needs of both parties are important, and we are all doing the best we can. None of us has to always say the correct thing to be supportive. The sensitivities and errors of the new widow will surely diminish over time, and we all can benefit from knowing how to better respond to loss.

As is evident from many of these essays, truisms are not necessarily helpful and generalities may undermine legitimate feelings. While logically we realize that we will get through this grief, for a new widow this future state seems far off in the distance. Although well-meaning, it is not always helpful to tell the new widow that things will get better, that our partner would have wanted us to be happy, that time cures all, or that we can still be grateful that the situation wasn't or isn't worse. Widows may not be ready to consider positive thoughts or outcomes while newly engrossed in grief. It is better to simply listen to her words and acknowledge how difficult this loss must be.

Besides listening, I found the most useful things other people did was check in and anticipate my needs. It is unlikely that a new grieving widow will reach out for emotional support, so she may rely on others to make initial efforts and specific offers. Even when she refuses or does not answer calls or emails, it is important to persist if you can. This checking-in needs to continue long after the one-year window has passed, as managing profound grief does not happen within a specified calendar. Each widow will have her own timetable, and each one will truly appreciate whatever support you can offer.

Acknowledgments

I WOULD LIKE to acknowledge my family and friends who have joined me on this difficult journey. Your love and friendship has been more than appreciated. You have continued to support me in spite of my ongoing struggles. My adult children, Dana and Michael, have become my best friends, and my close friends have become even closer. You know who you are.

Thank you also to those who encouraged me to write down my thoughts and feelings when I faced these interpersonal dilemmas. Several of you read sections of this book and even more of you listened kindly to my descriptions of social awkwardness and some of my problematic solutions. I appreciate your patience and your understanding.

I also want to thank my editor and writing coach Wayne South Smith for his wisdom and feedback in composing and organizing these essays, and for believing this was a worthwhile project.

Finally, I'd like to acknowledge the other widows who shared with me their personal challenges in managing this complicated life transition.

About the Author

EILEEN L. COOLEY earned her doctorate at Emory University and has been a licensed psychologist in Georgia for over 25 years. In her clinical psychology practice, she works with individuals and couples experiencing stress, depression, anxiety, and relationship concerns. She has conducted workshops on life transitions, stress management, and communication.

Dr. Cooley is a Professor Emerita of Psychology at Agnes Scott College where she taught courses in Counseling, Abnormal Psychology, Psychological Assessment, and Life-span Development. She has written professional articles on social skills, depression, attachment styles, and retirement. She also authored a children's book, *Why Do My Feet Say YES When My Head Says NO?*

For more information or to contact Dr. Cooley, please visit www.eileencooleyphd.com.

48624881R00135

Made in the USA
San Bernardino, CA
01 May 2017